SADDLING
UP
ANYWAY

SADDLING UP ANYWAY

THE DANGEROUS LIVES OF OLD-TIME COWBOYS

PATRICK DEAREN

TWODOT®

GUILFORD, CONNECTICUT
HELENA, MONTANA

A · TWODOT® · BOOK

An imprint of The Rowman & Littlefield Publishing Group, Inc.
4501 Forbes Blvd., Ste. 200
Lanham, MD 20706
www.rowman.com
A registered trademark of The Rowman & Littlefield Publishing Group, Inc.

Distributed by NATIONAL BOOK NETWORK

First Taylor Trade Publishing edition 2006.
First TwoDot paperback edition 2018.

British Library Cataloguing in Publication Information available

The hardback edition of this book was previously cataloged by the Library of Congress as follows:

Library of Congress Cataloging-in-Publication Data

Dearen, Patrick.
   Saddling up anyway : the dangerous lives of old-time cowboys 1 Patrick Dearen.—1st
Taylor Trade Pub. ed.
      p. cm.
   Includes bibliographical references and index.
   1. Cowboys—West (U.S.) —Social life and customs. 2. Cowboys—West (U.S.) —
History. 3. Cowboys—West (U.S.) —Biography. 4. Ranch life—West (U.S.)
5. Oral history—West (U.S.) 6. West (U.S.)—Social life and customs. I. Title.
F596.D383   2006
978.0092'2—dc22   2005025248

ISBN: 978-1-58979-223-4 (cloth: alk. paper)
ISBN: 978-1-4930-3297-6 (paperback: alk paper)
ISBN: 978-1-4616-3592-5 (ebook)

∞™ The paper used in this publication meets the minimum requirements of American National Standard for Information Sciences—Permanence of Paper for Printed Library Materials, ANSI/NISO Z39.48-1992.

Printed in the United States of America

For Richard Galle, my compadre of so many trails

Contents

Cowboy Lingo

adios, Jesus (interjection): a way of saying goodbye permanently, as in death; in this sense, the common Mexican name *Jesus* is pronounced *Kuh-SOOS*.

auger (verb): to engage in lively conversation.

booger (verb): to frighten.

break in two (verb): to begin pitching; said of a horse.

bronc (noun): a gelding that is none too gentle.

bronc buster (noun): one who breaks horses for riding purposes.

bust a bronc (verb): the act of breaking a horse for riding.

case of loco (noun): the state of being crazy.

chaps (noun): protective leather coverings for a rider's legs; also known as leggings.

cheek (verb): to grip a bridle headstall and pull a horse's head to its shoulder in prelude to mounting.

chouse (verb): to stir up cattle unnecessarily; often used metaphorically.

clabberhead (verb): an unpredictable horse lacking common sense.

cold jaw (verb): to avoid the pressure of a bit and refuse a rider's command; said of a horse.

cowboy (verb): to perform the duties of a cowboy.

cut bedding (verb): to share a bedroll.

cut the figure eight (verb): to pitch in a twisting motion; said of a horse.

dally (verb): in roping, to secure a lariat to a saddle horn by wrapping it around two or three times, thus allowing for slippage; from the Spanish phrase *dar la vuelta*, or "give a turn."

drags (noun): the animals at the rear of a marching herd.

drover (noun): a cowboy who drives cattle.

eternal brand (noun): death.

eternal range (noun): heaven.

fence-rower (noun): a horse that leaps frenziedly from one side to the other; said of a pitching horse.

forefoot (verb): to fell an animal by roping its front legs.

fork (verb): to straddle a horse; a "forked" rider is a superb horseman.

frogging it out (verb): to punish a horse by a method such as clubbing it in the skull with a quirt handle.

gig (verb): to spur a horse.

great divide (noun): death.

greenhorn (noun): an inexperienced cowboy.

hackamore (noun): a halter with a headpiece similar to a bridle and a band above the horse's mouth in lieu of a bit.

high lonesome (noun): the remotest of locations.

leggings (noun): protective leather coverings for a rider's legs; also known as chaps.

make a kick (verb): to complain.

mill (verb): to move in a circle.

outfit (noun): a ranch; a group of cowhands engaged in a cattle drive.

outlaw (noun): a vicious and untamable horse or bovine.

peg (verb): to plant the feet in anticipation of an impact at the end of a lariat; said of a roping horse.

pigeon-winger (noun): a horse that pitches as it takes flight straight ahead; a "pigeon-winging" bronc is an animal that does this.

point (noun): the front of a marching herd; (verb): to perform the duties of a cowboy riding point.

polled (adjective): without horns.

pull leather (verb): to clutch any part of a saddle to stay astride a pitching horse.

remuda (noun): a saddle horse herd.

sand in his gizzard (noun): courage.

screw down (verb): to sit as deep as possible in the saddle and dig spurs into the cinch.

see snakes (verb): to respond nervously to imagined dangers; said of a horse.

sky fire (noun): lightning and other electrical displays.

snake-blood (noun): an incorrigible horse that will pitch to exhaustion and lie down.

spook (verb): to unnerve.

stompede (noun): a cowboy's way of saying *stampede*.

stove-up (adjective): physically disabled.

sun-fisher (noun): a horse that pitches by jumping to the side.

swallow his head (verb): to lower the head as a prelude to pitching; said of a horse.

top hand (noun): a cowboy respected for his experience and ability.

turn a cat (verb): to tumble.

tie hard and fast (verb): to secure a lariat firmly to a saddle horn by means of a figure eight knot.

vaquero (noun): a cowboy, especially one of Mexican descent.

waddy (noun): originally a temporary or "fill-in" cowboy, from the term *wad* or *wadding*, but later applied to any cowhand.

wiggler (noun): a horse that pitches by twisting its rear end in the air as it vaults forward to land on stiff forelegs.

wormy (adjective): infested with screwworms.

wrangler (noun): the cowboy responsible for looking after the saddle horse herd.

Finding the Stirrup

Courage is being scared to death and saddling up anyway.

—John Wayne

A dangerous bronc and a determined cowboy on the OR range in Arizona in 1909.
(E. E. Smith Collection, Nita Stewart Haley Memorial Library, Midland, Texas)

*D*eath was never far from a cowboy. He may have submerged the possibility in the youthful bluster of supposed invincibility, but every time a cowhand dug his boot into the stirrup, the ride could carry him to trail's very end.

On all sides, judgment came creeping like an angry, black fog, ready to engulf and shroud. Threat took numerous forms, all of them sudden, many of them inescapable. A cowboy of early days might have caught a *whooshing* arrow or exploding slug, or confronted a raging river ready to drag him to the depths. A cowhand of any era faced the everyday perils inherent in this most dangerous of professions—the flinty hoofs and devil horns of an outlaw steer, the crush of a half ton of fury in the guise of a saddle horse, the snap of a rope pulling taut with power great enough to sever digits. Too, threat loomed in the sky, manifesting itself with wicked displays of nature's wrath—rains that blinded and chilled, hail that pounded and fractured, lightning that rattled bones and deafened if it missed . . . or came with silent finality if it didn't.

Pulling rein at a forsaken grave bearing the inscription "Unknown" on the Goodnight-Loving Trail in Texas in 1869, Henry P. Kellogg had good reason to fear that the epitaph might soon be his own. "How I dread," the young drover wrote in his journal, "the idea of a death of this kind, away from home and friends."

Similar concerns weighed heavily on Oliver Loving, who, along with Charles Goodnight, popularized this cattle trail from the Brazos River to the hated Pecos and upstream beyond the then-boundaries of the United States. Wounded by Comanches and nearing death in New Mexico Territory in 1867, Loving whispered his deep regret that he would be "laid away in a foreign country."

Goodnight, with a cowboy's understanding, reassured his friend: He would return Loving's remains to Texas for burial. True to his word, Goodnight did exactly that, directing a funeral caval- cade back through dangerous Indian country and on to Loving's Weatherford, Texas home. A century and a half later, Loving's grave still endures with the peaceful dignity due a cowboy.

Whether destined to be remembered or forgotten, a cowhand clung to life with all the zeal with which he approached his trade. The most loyal of employees, he displayed a work ethic beyond re- proach, repeatedly putting his neck on the line for a mere dollar a day.

"The boys never made a kick," nineteenth-century drover Teddy Blue Abbott remembered in 1931. "Did you ever hear of a herd being lost or turned plum loose? The only way they could be lost was for the whole outfit to die, cook and all. As long as one man could set his horse, the herd was held. The men that owned the herd would quit long before the [cowhands] would even give it a thought."

Such were the old-time cowboys, these men who rode fearlessly through danger, eluding for a while that awful black fog that chased at the very hoofs of their barreling horses.

Horses Good, Mean, and Sorry

Give me a saddle with a good horse under me and plenty of riding.
You couldn't suit me better.

—Raymond Richardson, cowhand

Tom Ford and Claud Jefferies working with a bronc on the Matador Ranch in Texas in 1905 as an unidentified cowhand looks on. (E. E. Smith Collection, Nita Stewart Haley Memorial Library, Midland, Texas)

cowhand's greatest ally was also his most dangerous foe.

On foot, a cowboy was about as effective, said one old cowpuncher, as "a one-legged man at a butt-kicking." No matter his courage or determination, he was sure to come up short in any confrontation with ornery cow brutes of superior size, strength, stamina, and speed. What good were boots against flinty hoofs, or wits against deadly horns? What chance had a hundred and sixty pounds against a half ton?

"If you're not a-horseback," mused Southwestern cowboy Frank Yeary, "you might just as well be at the house." L. Kinser, a cowhand of the 1920s, echoed his sentiments: "You'd be up salt creek without your horse."

Indeed, once in the saddle, a ranch hand was transformed. No longer was he a mere man with insurmountable limitations and frailties; he was a knight of the range, possessing the speed to overtake stampeding beeves, the strength to throw a yearling at rope's end. He had the agility to outmaneuver a quick-footed steer intent on bolting, the endurance to keep pace with a herd marching relentlessly. He was part man, part animal, and all cowhand.

"An ol' boy would just as soon go off without his pants as go off without his horse," observed P. O. "Slim" Vines, who forked his share of broncs in the 1920s. "They're just part of you."

Working in tandem, man and horse accomplished what neither could have done on his own. For some cowhands, this awareness led to genuine respect for the horses in his mount. When eighty-seven-year-old Walton Poage died in 1995 after a full, rich life on the range and in the rodeo arena, his newspaper obituary included the fact that he had been preceded in death not only by his wife and parents, but by someone named Dan. Only in the case of a caring cowboy would surviving family members pay such tribute to the one most responsible for making him what he had been.

Dan was Poage's horse.

"I believe that's the best friend you got, if you get to looking at it right—a horse and a dog," reflected Leonard Hernandez, a South Texas cowpuncher by 1920.

To a less sensitive cowhand, however, an outfit's horses were pieces of machinery to be used and abused as he saw fit. He might ride an undesirable pony to exhaustion and then spur it in the shoulders, intentionally crippling it to avoid drawing the animal again. Without cause, he might club a bronc in the skull with an iron-loaded quirt handle, or whip it in the face with a leather strap or the double of a rope and risk blinding an eye. Even after the ride was over, a horse faced punishment at his hand; should the animal bow up as he unsaddled it, he might lash it with the bridle reins. In riders and horses alike, the range nurtured all types of personalities, not all of them exemplary.

"Horses are just like people," opined Seth Young, a cowboy by 1910. "There's good ones, and mean ones, and sorry ones."

No matter a cowhand's regard for his horse, one thing was certain: His very life hung in the balance anytime he was in the saddle. In so many ways, cow ponies could be catalysts for disaster, dooming their riders to stove-up lives or worse. Horses' often volatile natures (from spirited to snake-blood), sheer size (up to twelve hundred pounds), and speed (thirty-five or more miles per hour) were ingredients for catastrophe. Moreover, cowhands plied their trade in an unpredictable environment that often demanded instantaneous decisions. As if on a field of war, horses and riders had to react instinctively to fluid events beyond their control, whether they involved turf or beeves or raging storms.

Ninety-five percent of a cowhand's success may have rested in his horse, but an equal percentage of his accidents also stemmed from hugging a saddle. An ally and foe, indeed, was the cow pony.

"You've got to use your head or you'll get hurt bad," warned W. R. Green, a cowhand of the early 1900s.

Trouble brewed as soon as a cowboy tried to break a gelding, the first step in developing a cow horse.

"Two or three of you would hold him till you get a saddle on him, put a blindfold on him so he couldn't see," recalled Lonnie Griffith, a cowboy by 1915. "If them horses could see you, why, they was liable to kick you. Whenever you got up there in that saddle, boy, it was all up to you."

Assuredly, as soon as a cowboy's weight hit leather, the bronc would "break in two," pitching with a tornado-like fury that rattled bones and jarred teeth.

"If you was a good rider, why, you could usually stay on him," remembered Will Durham, who began cowboying in 1899. "If you

Monclavio Lucero busting a bronc on the LS Ranch in Texas in 1907. (E. E. Smith Collection, Nita Stewart Haley Memorial Library, Midland, Texas)

weren't, you'd usually grab for the saddle horn and catch yourself in the seat of the britches about the time you hit the ground."

Using a variety of bucking tactics, a horse could not only addle a man, but dismantle his saddle. A "pigeon-winging" bronc took flight straight ahead, while a "sun-fisher" jumped to one side and a "fence-rower" leaped frenziedly from one side to the other. Toughest to master was a "wiggler," which twisted its rear end in the air as it vaulted forward to land on stiff forelegs.

"The rider who could stay on a wiggler," observed Sam J. Rogers, a Pecos River horse breaker of the 1890s, "had the staying ability of a leach."

James Cape, a cowboy of the 1800s, was even more colorful in his assessment: "Some [horses] am just natural pitchers and can do the hoochy-koochy while in the air. . . . Sometimes such horses makes the stars come right down in front of you."

Without question, the jarring impact of hoofs against turf wreaked physiological havoc with every bronc buster. "Many times I'd ride 'em till I had the nosebleed so bad I'd get weak, and my guts would seem to be about ready to bust out," recalled L. E. Smith, who first saddled up in Central Texas in the 1880s.

"If you happen to have your mouth open," added Rogers, "you'll just about bust your jaw bone when your jaws pop together. I once saw a bronc buster bite his tongue so bad he couldn't talk for weeks. It's just like somebody going to your chin with his fist."

A horse breaker also paid the price for clinching his knees about a bronc, an absolute necessity in weathering the fury. At every wrinkle in his pants, friction would peel the skin and bloody his leg.

"My shins . . . would be plum raw all the time I worked with them horses," said Smith.

Broken bones and concussions were all too common, and few horse breakers came away unscathed. John L. Murrell, busting an eleven-hundred-pound gelding of Percheron-Steel Dust lineage in the early 1930s, clung to the saddle until the horse crashed into the corral fence. The collision broke his nose and knocked him unconscious.

"I was out from about eight o'clock in the morning till after dark," he recalled.

Sometimes, onlookers were forced to extreme measures to save a bronc buster's life. J. P. Benard, breaking a horse on his father's Texas ranch in the 1880s, remained in control until the animal made a twisting jump. Thrown hard, Benard lay helpless as the bronc turned to crush him with its hoofs.

"I was flat on my stomach with the wind knocked out of me, and the horse could have easily stomped me flatter than a hot cake if Dad hadn't've shot him," he related.

The long-term effects of busting broncs were dramatic and sometimes tragic.

"I hurt all over, all the time," lamented fifty-four-year-old J. M. Brown during the Great Depression. He had first hired out as a bronc buster in 1899 on a ranch fifteen miles north of Fort Worth. "I'm just like a punch-drunk prizefighter. . . . After a bronc buster gets thrown once, real good, as a rule he's good for nothing else but a three-by-six hole in the ground. . . . I've been thrown so many times that I'm just cheating the undertaker by living."

Even if broken to the saddle, few ranch horses ever became gentle. On the contrary, most were "crazy as hell," said cowhand Bill Davidson.

"They'd kick you or paw you or buck you off," elaborated L. Kinser. "You had to be awake all the time."

Steve "Slim" Armentrout learned such a lesson the hard way in the early 1930s when he casually walked behind his horse to flush a coyote from the West Texas brush. Suddenly the bronc's rear hoofs exploded into his stomach with punishing force. Felled, Armentrout

Bronc buster Monclavio Lucero getting thrown on the LS Ranch in Texas in 1907. (E. E. Smith Collection, Nita Stewart Haley Memorial Library, Midland, Texas)

writhed and moaned as he feared for his well-being. "I thought at first I was hurt pretty bad," he remembered.

Finally dragging himself up and crawling on the sorrel, Armentrout whipped the animal into a hard gallop for the ranch house. Fortunately, his injury wasn't serious, and he was back on the job as soon as the swelling subsided.

A cowhand wise to the ways of horses knew what to expect when a foreman asked which animal he wanted for his first day. "Give me the worst SB you got," Fin Cox once told a new boss, "'cause I know I'm gonna get him anyway."

Merely saddling a high-strung horse for a morning's work was problem enough, especially if it was an outlaw that would sooner kill than cooperate. Charles K. Smith, who cowboyed on the Charco de los Marinos Ranch in West Texas in the early 1900s, concluded that even good breeding couldn't erase a "case of loco" in a thoroughbred-cross named Clabber.

"He had the nastiest disposition of any horse I ever rode," charged Smith. "He never did pitch, but he'd paw you. I was walking up, putting my bridle on him, and he reared up and pawed me. I got my head out of the way, but he hit me in the back. He nearly tore my shirt off."

Sometimes a cowboy had to tie up a bronc's hind foot just to secure a saddle; otherwise, he faced an impossible situation. Fred McClellan, a 1920s hand on the Spade Ranch in Texas, remembered a horse named "Jesse James" that had earned its moniker for good reason.

"Invariably when you'd throw that blanket and saddle on, he'd just bawl and buck that saddle off before you could get it cinched up," he recalled.

A cowhand often kept the girt loose at first, allowing the animal to accommodate gradually to the thirty-three pounds of leather.

"If they don't like that saddle, they'll just bow up their back when you cinch them up," explained Slim Vines. "That's when they'll buck most of the time, if they'll buck at all. If you'll lead them around the pen and holler at them and keep them scared, then they'll get that hump out of their back."

After snugging the girt, a cowhand in a corral might release a bronc and let it "pitch to the saddle." Even as the horse calmed, a prudent cowboy made sure to open the gate, a precaution should the animal bolt with him. As Shorty Northcutt of Texas once said, "I could take the pitch out of 'em. I couldn't take the run out of 'em."

Finally, a cowhand was ready to climb on—one of the most dangerous moments in a cowpuncher's day. With broncs, it was essential to "cheek" the animal, a procedure in which a cowboy gripped the bridle headstall and pulled the horse's head to its shoulder. With a simultaneous hold on the saddle horn, the cowhand now had a measure of control, for a pony couldn't buck without burying its head between its legs.

The consequences of not cheeking could be severe. Louis Baker, a cowboy by 1910, could never forget a gelding named "Ol' Kicker," a horse notorious for kicking viciously unless a cowboy pulled its head around. Gaston Boykin, who broke his first bronc by 1920, once saw a horse rip a cowboy's stout leggings with a slashing hoof. On another occasion, Boykin himself narrowly escaped injury when he failed to cheek a two-year-old mare on the Shanghai Pierce spread in South Texas.

"As fast as I left the ground, it just turned and threw me hard and fast," he recalled. "The top of my boot hung in the stirrup."

Dangling from the opposite side, Boykin was in dire straits, for his head was only a foot off the ground. Luckily, his Great Dane came to his rescue, clamping its powerful jaws on the horse's snout and ending the fray. "Saved my life," he reflected.

A waddy named Chapo, who rode with Boykin on Miller brothers holdings in Texas, wasn't so fortunate. Oblivious to the dangers, Chapo never bothered to cheek a horse. When fellow punchers found him dead, the victim of a hoof to the skull, they gained added respect for cheeking.

Even if a cowhand did everything right, mounting a bronc remained treacherous.

"You had to get on one real quick," said McClellan. "Some of them would start bucking before you'd get in the saddle."

"I asked a wild horse man in the 1930s how he got on them tall horses," related Fish Wilson of the Texas Panhandle. "He said, 'Put your knee in his shoulder and kick a-flyin'.'"

In his haste to get astride, however, a rider might make a careless mistake. Louis Baker, anxious to pursue horses escaping from a West Texas corral about 1924, ran out and seized his saddled bronc. As he swung his leg over, his boot struck the horse's neck.

"Boy, he swallowed his head and jumped," Baker related. "First thing I knew, the saddle horn was behind me."

Slammed to the turf, Baker got up "a-cussin' and a-cryin'" and climbed back on. "Boy, I was eating him up with them spurs. I rode up there, 'Now, you dirt son of—!' When he got through bucking, I seen four girls sitting out there in a car, watching me, dying laughing. I just tipped my hat to them and took off a-runnin'."

William A. Smith, who rode the North Texas range in the 1880s and 1890s, proved that even a swift and mistake-free mount wasn't always enough.

"I got seated and turned that critter's head loose," he said of one horse. "When I did there was an explosion. That critter went up high and wiggled out from under me, faster than a hell-diver goes under water. He left me in the air with nothing to sit on."

At all costs, a rider had to stay on his feet when trying to mount, for a prone cowboy was vulnerable to attack. John L. Murrell, readying to fork a horse on the Mashed O Ranch in the Texas Panhandle, found lethal hoofs in his face when the animal knocked him flat. "I guess he hit me over the ear with one foot, 'cause I had a gash just over my ear," he related. "I come to about five miles from there, laying under a wagon. They said they caught the horse and brought him back to me and I got on him, but I never did know it."

A similar situation proved especially serious in 1930 after drovers bedded a cattle herd for the night near a bootlegging joint west of Midland, Texas. By daybreak, most of the drovers were drunk and in no condition to cope with skittish broncs. One of the few sober hands, Slim Vines, watched a staggering cowboy try to mount his horse.

"It jumped out from under him and his foot hung in the stirrup and it started dragging him," remembered Vines. "It kicked him on the side of the head, laying his scalp over on one side before he got loose."

Cowhands had to flag down a passing motorist in order to transport the injured man to a Midland doctor.

Booze and broncs were seldom a good mix, but even a sober cowboy faced peril with a horse that jumped or reared as he sought the saddle. Twice, top hand Slim Armentrout sustained a broken ankle under a crushing hoof. Another hard-riding cowboy, Fish Wilson, suffered permanent injury to his hip and arm in the 1960s when a rearing horse fell while his foot was in the stirrup.

"That's the scariest thing that can happen to you—a horse rearing over backwards," noted 1920s cowhand Paul Patterson.

With broncs prone to wheel as a rider attempted to mount, Tom Parisher of Texas learned to position his horse against a tree to keep it from spinning away. "If he whirled toward me, I could get on him and ride him," Parisher explained. "But if he went the other way, he might buck me off."

Getting caught by a whirling horse was a desperate situation that

A horse falling back with its rider in the 1910s, probably on the SMS Ranch in Texas. Photo by Frank Reeves, *The Story of the SMS Ranch*, 1919. (E. E. Smith Collection, Nita Stewart Haley Memorial Library, Midland, Texas)

no cowpuncher relished, but even decades of experience couldn't grant immunity. In Borden County, Texas, in the late 1970s, septuagenarian Vance Davis tried to mount a bronc that another rider had declined. "I was hung to the stirrup," recalled Davis. "He got me about two feet off the ground and he was whirling, and I was up in the air going around and around. He was kicking at me but never did hit me. When I finally come out, I just hit the ground rolling."

If a cowboy finally did manage to straddle a bronc, a rodeo usually erupted.

"He'd leave the ground when you do," said Olan George, who first hired out in Trans-Pecos Texas in 1924. "Some of them just pitched for the fun of it. They weren't mean, just cold-shouldered. On a chilly morning, you didn't break that horse off in a lope, because he would pitch every time. He had to have that warm-up."

Still, a slow-paced mile and a little lather didn't always discourage a horse from pitching when urged to greater speed.

Sometimes a cowhand might loosen a horse by galloping it around a corral, but even under controlled conditions, a pitching bronc could get a cowboy in trouble. On a West Texas ranch in 1936, twenty-nine-year-old Lewis Doran endured the frenetic jumps of a bay until his stirrup caught a protruding post. The impact slung Doran's foot back and boogered the horse even more.

"I went right over his head, and both them spurs just went in the ground," said Doran, who suffered a thigh injury.

All in all, getting in the saddle and facing a bronc's initial rebellion posed such grave risks that some cowboys even stayed in the stirrups to urinate. Like Rube Barnett of the XIT in Texas, they knew they had reason to sing "Farewell, Pretty Mary" every time they cheeked an unruly animal—and they had plenty to cheek every doggoned day.

Sky-Kicking Broncs

A cowpuncher. . . . That was what I was born for—had it in my blood and couldn't get it out.

—T. E. Hines, cowhand

Henry Lyman on a high-flying bronc on the LS Ranch in Texas in 1907. (E. E. Smith Collection, Nita Stewart Haley Memorial Library, Midland, Texas)

Some cowhands considered a fighting nature in a bronc an attribute. "A healthy joyous life, to be on a spirited horse!" wrote Edward G. Hayes from a Colorado ranch on May 5, 1887. Frank Yeary, who cut his cowboy teeth thirty-five years later in Texas, put it less poetically: "A damned horse won't pitch, he ain't worth havin'."

Judged by Yeary's standard, cowhands were seldom at a loss for worthy horses, which demanded the best in a rider's strength, stamina, and wiles. He could never relax, for a bronc could find numerous reasons in a half-day's ride to "cut the figure eight." The animal might be a snake-blood, an incorrigible outlaw that would pitch till exhaustion and lie down. It might "see snakes," mistaking a stick or the rustling of a bush for a rattler ready to strike. Perhaps its belly or flanks would be sensitive to a protruding limb or the gig of a spur, or maybe it simply disliked its rider.

Although horses sometimes pitched without notice, an astute cowhand learned to read specific warning signs. Often, he could feel the animal tense like a coiled spring and develop a mad-cat hump in its back. If the ears flared and the head started to drop between the knees, he could try to "hold him up" by pulling on the reins and leaning backward. For added leverage, he might use his free hand to push against the saddle horn. Once a rider tilted forward, he had lost the battle and was left with no choice but to "screw down" for a ride to Jericho.

Generally, a cowpuncher preferred a saddle with a deep swell that hugged his loins and made him more difficult to dislodge. Slim Armentrout had an S. D. Meyers saddle with an eighteen-inch swell and fourteen-inch seat. "It was just all I could do to screw down in that thing," he noted, "but when you got down in it, you could ride about anything that had hair on it."

As a bronc turned dust devil, bawling like a wild bull and jumping for the moon, the rider might "pull leather," clutching any part of the saddle he could. Not only did he have to keep his balance and anticipate every move, he also had to show the animal who was boss. Even for cowboys who respected their horses, this was a time for "frogging it out" with a quirt or for relentlessly spurring its belly or shoulders. A rider couldn't hesitate or display fear, for to do so would only embolden a horse already trying to send him sky-high.

"If that horse ever pitches," instructed a 1920s rancher in regard to a dreaded bronc named Bald Hornet, "you just do whatever you're big enough to."

One thing was certain—a cowboy astride a clabberhead was useless in a cattle operation. Observed Frank Derrick, a 1930s cowhand: "With lots of young boys who'd go to work on a ranch, [the foreman] would ask him what kind of hand he is, and he'd say, 'Well, what kind of horses you gonna furnish me?' You can't depend on a man that's fighting his horse every time he's trying to do something. He's in your way, and he's in trouble, too."

At one time or another, every cowhand ate dirt at the hoofs of a pitching horse. "The cowboy that said he never was throwed—by gosh, he never did ride much," said Alton Davis, a Texas Hill Country waddy by 1920. Even if a rider stayed astride, he might grimace in agony at some unforeseen calamity. In 1938, thirty-six-year-old Otis Coggins broke his arm when a sky-jumping Texas bronc drove him into a mesquite tree. Lewis Doran, diving from a pitching horse in the Ozona country of Texas in 1968, cracked five ribs against a mesquite.

The ground, though, could wreak the greatest harm. J. R. "Jim" Stroup, riding a troublesome horse in the Texas Panhandle about 1957, kept his guard up throughout most of an afternoon, but as he took the animal down a riverbank, he erred by relaxing in the saddle.

"I was thrown about as high as I ever was in my life, and flat on my back," he remembered. "He jumped on me and pawed me, but he missed."

Unable to walk, Stroup dragged himself a quarter-mile to a ranch house and spent the next four days in a hospital.

Walter Boren, who cowboyed in Texas and Oklahoma, also once paid a price for inattention when he dozed and spurred his horse in the flank. The hard-packed ground flew up and numbed his leg, forcing him to summon help and gain medical treatment.

Rugged hills always heightened the dangers of a pitching horse, for the gravedigger seemed to haunt every hazardous slope and line of rimrock. Few riders lived to tell a more harrowing tale than Green Mankin, a West Texas cowboy who swung astride a bronc named Greasewood one morning in the 1920s.

"He was a crazy horse—when he got mad and hot, he'd try to kill hisself or kill you," he remembered.

Mankin, however, was never one to back away from a challenge. He had such grit and daring, in fact, that he would have "charged hell with a gallon of water," as one old cowhand described him. But as Mankin reined Greasewood about for the day's work on a cedary Pecos divide rimmed by precipice, he suddenly found his water bucket leaking ominously, while hell burned hotter than ever.

"That ol' horse throwed his head down and went to pitching and running for that caprock," Mankin lamented.

Another cowhand desperately turned his horse in the runaway's path, but Greasewood knocked the animal "sky-western crooked" and continued its hell-bent dash for a twelve-foot cliff. Related Mankin:

"That ol' horse didn't slack up. We went right over the caprock. That's one time I give up—I thought that was the end of the trail."

Incredibly, Mankin's animal crashed through a huge cedar below, splintered a thick limb, and landed on its feet on the mountain's steep slope.

"It took all the hair off his right hip, but that horse never stumbled," he continued. "He just pitched plum' two or three hundred yards down that hill and didn't stagger anytime. I felt like I could've rode any horse then."

Back at the summit, shaken cowboys pulled rein at cliff's edge to stare in awe at Mankin's hairbreadth escape. All too often, cowhands knew only grief and regret in such a situation.

When Texas hand Allen Robinson didn't return to the wagon on time in the late 1920s or early 1930s, Mankin and Gaston Boykin rode in search. In the churned rubble and broken limbs on a precipitous slope under rimrock, they read the grim story of a hellcat bronc throwing a rider into a dead cedar. Underneath, they found flies blowing Robinson's blood-caked body; a razor-sharp snag had slashed his jugular vein and opened a fatal torrent.

"He had pulled off his shirt and tried to stop the blood, but he couldn't," remembered Boykin.

Sometimes, even preemptive measures on a mountain weren't enough to ward off death. In 1932, Charlie Drennan kept close watch on a fellow rider's unruly black horse as their animals struggled up an insidious West Texas grade. When the black began to buck, Drennan brought his horse abreast to discourage it from turning, but the black still managed to wheel and start downhill. Suddenly the horse went down and rolled with its rider, fatally crushing him.

"He didn't ever know what struck him," said Drennan.

Sure-footed mules could also endanger a cowboy in rimrock country—even if he stayed in the stirrups as Tom Parisher did about 1929. As the Texas cowhand took a mule down treacherous Lancaster Hill on the lower Pecos, his saddle slipped forward and spooked the animal.

"He went to pitching and throwed me, saddle and all," recounted Parisher. "I hit down in front of him and still had my feet in the stirrups."

A cowhand ascending a treacherous bluff in the early 1900s. (E. E. Smith Collection, Nita Stewart Haley Memorial Library, Midland, Texas)

The heights always demanded that a rider be on guard, no matter how well-behaved a horse might be. Orval Sparks, riding the Concho River in West Texas about 1945, never suspected the steep bank was undercut until it collapsed and sent horse and rider plunging fifteen feet to the water. Fortunately, the river provided a soft landing, but the situation involving Seth Young of the Texas Hill Country in the late 1910s was far more ominous. Riding along ever-narrowing rimrock, with an unscalable bluff on one side and a sheer drop on the other, Young realized too late that he was in trouble. There was scarce enough room to turn the horse, but he nevertheless tried. Suddenly the animal lost its footing and fell hard, spilling the cowhand.

"When I hit the ground, I was a-crawlin' and a-pawin' to keep him from rollin' on top of me," recalled Young, who barely avoided serious injury.

Whether on a slope or a flat, any pitching episode increased the chances of a saddle animal falling—a dreaded event in a cowhand's life. A half ton of horseflesh and a brick wall of earth were a deadly combination to a rider caught between. "I'd rather a horse throw me off anytime than fall with me," declared Tyson Midkiff, a cowboy by 1907.

Jim Witt, astride a sun-fishing bronc on a Pecos River ranch about 1928, took the best the animal had to offer until it fell and crushed his leg. "It looked like a stove pipe for about a month," he recalled. During the same era, a similar fall in the Big Bend of Texas hobbled W. R. Green so severely that a doctor warned him not to ride for a full year—a blow to any cowboy born to the saddle.

As if a catapulting bronc wasn't threat enough, many other factors could also drag a rider from his perch. If a waddy packed an unnecessary Winchester on his saddle, a hooking limb might yank rifle and cowhand alike from a running horse, as happened to Jim Stroup about 1920. If a rider let a loping horse take him under a clothesline, as Louis Baker once did, he usually met with a startling stop that sent him flying. If a roper guessed wrong as his striding horse dodged an obstacle, he might land in a deep sleep and never awaken—the very epitaph of one rider during a sheep roundup in Terrell County, Texas, in 1934. Focused on roping a fugitive lamb, the Moseur and Mendel cowhand relied on instinct when a cedar sprang up in the path of his barreling horse. He leaned in anticipation, but his horse veered in the opposite direction and pulled the saddle out from under him.

"When I first saw him, he was layin' flat on his back," remembered Tom Parisher, who was sixty yards away. "He raised one leg up, and that's the only time he ever moved. By the time we got to him, he was dead."

Even the act of dismounting could be perilous, judging by Fred McClellan's mishap sometime before 1947. Galloping his horse up to a closed gate, the West Texas cowhand began stepping off as he pulled rein. When the swing of his leg frightened the bronc, the animal dodged and slung him under the fence.

But merely remaining in the saddle wasn't always enough to elude harm, especially astride a running horse in Texas mesquites. About 1930, for example, Carl Lane sustained a crippling thorn in his knee as he pursued fleeing broncs. Fellow Texan Otis Coggins, fending off slapping limbs during the same era, took a massive thorn completely through a wrist protected by heavy gloves. Left to fester, a mesquite thorn could poison a victim, but Coggins suffered through an entire month before a doctor cut it out.

Even if brush complied and horses cooperated, at every stride waited snares to fell a bronc and maybe cripple its rider. "It wasn't awful uncommon for every horse you had to fall with you," remembered Shorty Northcutt, who endured his share of mishaps on the Spade Ranch in West Texas.

In any wreck, a horse slammed into the turf in one of three directions—left, right, or straight ahead. The latter was the most dangerous, for momentum would drive a rider over its head and leave him vulnerable as the animal somersaulted across him. Paradoxically, the slower a horse's gait, the greater the chance of serious injury—a lesson that only experience could convey.

As a young cowhand in Texas, Slim Vines watched with concern as Scharbauer Ranch foreman John Dublin kept his horse in a gallop across a pasture riddled with pitfalls. Vines knew that Dublin was a seasoned hand; why would he take such a risk?

"John," Vines told him later, "you're gonna hit a hole sometime and get killed."

"Naw," Dublin explained, "you don't want to slow-lope a horse around—the faster they go, the further they'll roll you. If he falls, he'll throw you away from him and never get on top of you."

By stepping off a falling animal, an agile cowboy could aid his own cause in distancing himself from an accident. It was a skill that demanded not only athleticism and presence of mind, but a position in the saddle that would allow him to escape quickly. Success began with proper stirrup length.

When 1800s cowhand Beverly Greenwood saw young Thomas J. Henderson limping after repeated horse falls in the Chihuahuan Desert of Texas in 1924, the old-timer immediately recognized the problem.

"Son, you're gonna get killed riding with long stirrups."

"How come, Mr. Bev?" asked Henderson.

"You can't get out of that saddle if a horse is falling with you, can you?"

"Hell, no," Henderson admitted. "You have to ride him to the ground."

Greenwood proceeded to give Henderson sage advice: adjust his stirrups so he could clear the saddle by two handbreadths as he stood to dismount in an emergency.

Although a cowboy might quit a horse to either side, circumstances sometimes demanded that he do so directly over the animal's head. Slim Vines, galloping a bronc named Widow Maker across a Texas ranch in the early 1930s, had to react instinctively when the pony suddenly dropped to its breast and plowed through the dirt.

"I'd pulled my feet out of the stirrups—I knew he was going down just as soon as he stumbled," Vines recalled. "When he got low enough, my feet hit the ground. I pushed myself out and just run off out in front of him."

Whirling, Vines saw an ominous sight. "Here come his ol' rear end over, hitting right behind me. If I'd've gone down still in that saddle, he'd've hit me right in the back."

A cowhand needed to seize every such advantage, for a bronc was just a wreck waiting to happen.

What Made 'em Fall

My legs are so bowed you could use them for barrel hoops.

—Eddie McGregor, cowhand

Turkey Track cowboys rushing to the aid of a downed rider on the Texas prairie in 1906.
(E. E. Smith Collection, Nita Stewart Haley Memorial Library, Midland, Texas)

Sometimes the trap that felled a horse remained unidentified, even as the accident hobbled a cowboy for a week or a lifetime. Perhaps he grimaced at a cantle driving into his back, as Texas cowhand Gid Reding did in 1926, or writhed to a broken collarbone and leg like Tom Blasingame in the Texas Panhandle in 1955. It might be a fractured hand that dealt him misery, as with Claude Owens in Trans-Pecos Texas in the late 1920s, or maybe a crippled hip invited arthritis, the factor that eventually confined Texas cowhand Leonard Proctor to a wheelchair. In a profession without safety helmets, a head injury might rob a rider of even the memory of a wreck, along with all knowledge of its cause.

Hudson "Bud" Mayes, riding upon a West Texas windmill to join a long-ago roundup, wasn't even aware that his horse had fallen on the way. But his glazed eyes and bleeding face told fellow cowhands all they needed to know. They pulled him off his pony and helped him to the mill.

"I didn't know nothing till they was letting water pump on my head," Mayes reflected.

In today's high-tech world, Mayes might have been airlifted to a medical center for evaluation and a lengthy stay. But on a forsaken range where a man had to be tough or die, waddies simply put the addled cowhand on a gentle bay and trusted it to carry him home alone.

John Patterson suffered even greater head trauma when his horse fell for unknown reasons in hard-packed West Texas sand in 1924. Knocked unconscious, Patterson stayed in a coma ten days, even as a skilled nurse tended him in a region void of hospitals. He wandered in and out of consciousness another three weeks, bleeding at the ears from a swollen brain. Although he eventually recovered to climb back in the saddle, he never regained memory of the wreck that almost killed him.

Sometimes a horse fall of unknown cause forced a lone cowboy to extraordinary measures just to survive. West Texas cowpuncher Ted Sorrells, for example, had to crawl two miles and ford a frozen river after a 1940s accident.

Merely knowing what triggered a mishap, however, could do nothing at the time to ward off injury. A running horse might simply stumble on rocks and go down, a calamity that led to torn cartilage in Thomas Henderson's rib cage sometime before 1924.

"I went right over his head," recounted the Texas cowhand, whose long stirrups prevented a controlled exit. "That SOB hit the ground and rolled plum' over me. And I just thought, 'Oh man, does this hurt!'"

Sometimes, unfamiliar terrain was the culprit. Paul Patterson, riding a horse and leading a second animal by hackamore rope tied to the saddle horn, never expected trouble in the mid-1920s as he started across Flat Rock, a sprawling shelf of West Texas limestone. When the trailing bronc spooked and jerked the rope, Patterson's mount lost its footing on the slick surface and crashed to its side.

"I was riding a saddle with a big ol' swell fork—that's all that kept me from breaking my leg," said Patterson.

Pinned, he could only let the horse try to regain its feet and free him. Suddenly, he realized just how grave his situation really was.

"Every time he'd flop to get up, it would scare this bronc, and he'd jerk him back down on me," he remembered. "I thought, 'This is it.'"

Unable to reach his pocketknife to cut the hackamore rein, Patterson had only one choice: try to calm the bronc with gentle words. After what seemed an eternity, the bronc finally edged closer, allowing the saddle horse to rise and Patterson to escape.

Sometimes, native vegetation could upend a horse, especially in a harried chase. Pursuing stampeding mares in the Big Bend of Texas one long-ago morning, Clarence Arrott rode hard through Chihuahuan Desert shrubs.

"My horse went to jump over one of 'em and it tangled in his feet and throwed him," Arrott recalled. "I saw stars for an hour or two—it knocked me out."

Bill Townsend, similarly running his horse through West Texas brush in 1931, fractured his back when a low-lying mesquite limb jumped up in the animal's path.

"It caught that ol' pony just above the knees just like you'd forefooted him with a rope," he narrated. "Boy, he turned over. I got up and started to crawl out of the way, and he come over on top of me."

Fortunately, the horse stood still after gaining its feet, allowing Townsend to drag himself over, climb on, and ride for help at a nearby corral.

A saddle pony was large and powerful, but so were beeves and free-ranging horses, a fact that created the potential for disastrous collisions. To a rider such as Douglas Poage of the OH Triangle in Texas, the outcome could be painful. As the fifteen-year-old chased a runaway animal in 1922, a cow darted in his path, forcing his horse to try to hurdle it. When the pony tripped, the unyielding ground delivered a bone-snapping blow to his arm.

Billy Rankin, fearlessly riding into a herd of wild mares on the lower Pecos River before 1934, fared no better; three mares ran over his pony and spilled him to the alkali. As clubbing hoofs flashed, the stunned hand could only wallow helplessly with permanently injured knees. Luckily, another cowboy was on hand to ride in and rescue him.

One of the most amazing escapes after a collision came in 1921 in a Texas Hill Country incident involving a fleeing heifer and a pursuing cowboy. Si Loeffler's horse, Question Mark, was a good cow pony, but the black animal was also stubborn enough at times to "cold jaw"—ignore the pressure of the bit and go where it wanted. Now, as Question Mark bolted in the wrong direction,

Loeffler jerked the reins violently. The force pulled the bit entirely out of the pony's mouth, but at least Loeffler succeeded in wheeling the black.

"Boy, that ol' horse was mad," he recounted. "I busted him with the quirt and made him get after that heifer."

Question Mark was in a full run up a steep grade leading to a three-foot ledge rising perpendicularly. Jutting back into the rock shelf was a narrow inverted V of open space. This was a time for quick action on the black's part, but instead of trying to head off the heifer, the angry horse simply ran over it.

The impact dropped both animals and hurled Loeffler from the saddle. In an instant the ledge was a sledgehammer driving toward his skull. Even if he avoided a direct hit, at his heels were a thousand pounds of tumbling horse threatening to crush him against solid rock.

Suddenly Providence stepped in.

"I just lit right in that V-shape of those rocks," Loeffler remembered. "When that horse quit rolling, he was laying right on top of me—I could see the seat of my saddle. I thought, 'Now what if he slips down and gets on me!'"

Tucked in the V's recesses, Loeffler could only watch helplessly as the upside-down horse struggled frantically just inches above. After anxious moments, the addled black finally freed itself, allowing the awed cowboy to crawl out of his unlikely refuge.

The most fiendish perpetrator of a horse wreck was a hidden depression in the turf—perhaps an eroded cow trail or hand-dug well, or maybe a sinkhole or animal burrow. When a flying hoof dropped abruptly, a crushing fall was almost inevitable, leaving a cowboy's destiny to chance. If he was lucky, only his pride might be bruised, as with thirteen-year-old wrangler Bill Eddins in Trans-Pecos Texas in 1914.

"I was ridin' a little ol' high-strung horse, and it had his head right up in my face," Eddins said of his barreling animal. "I looked down and he was just fixin' to step off in a dug well, five or six feet deep."

Eddins frantically pulled rein and tried to wheel the bronc, but it nevertheless slipped backward into the muddy abyss.

"I was sure scared," recalled Eddins, who climbed out and walked to camp. "I told everybody I rode a horse off in a dug well. They went to teasin' me, and I started to bawling. It took half a day to dig my horse out."

A rutted cow trail in the Texas Panhandle did more than embarrass Tom Blasingame in the early 1960s; when his pony "turned a cat," the JA cowhand broke his collarbone and lost consciousness. Upon regaining his senses, Blasingame had no choice but to walk three miles back to his line camp.

Small sinkholes were particularly worrisome to a rider. Texas cowhand Fred McClellan, spurring his horse after runaways one morning in 1932, flew a dozen feet and struck his head when pockmarked turf seized a lunging hoof. He struggled up and staggered to his bronc, only to collapse into oblivion as blood oozed from his ears and nose. Several anxious hours passed before McClellan was out of the woods.

"I had a hell of a headache when I come to in the hospital that evening," he remembered a half-century later.

Sometimes a sinkhole foreshadowed a deep-six excavation from which no cowboy ever walked away. One tragic morning on the 7D in Texas, a wormy cow lured a cowhand on a frantic ride across a pitted lake bed. Suddenly the bronc's forefeet sank, precipitating a violent wreck that took a frightful toll on the man's thoracic cavity. When his horse returned alone to the bunkhouse, 7D cowhands rode in search and found him alive, but he would die of his injuries within a year or so.

Rivaling sinkholes for peril in a cowboy's life were badger burrows, for they were large enough to swallow both forefeet of a horse.

"The worst fall I ever got was from a badger hole," contended Charles K. Smith, who was knocked senseless when his horse somersaulted in a late-1910s accident. Olan George, punching cows for a Texas outfit in 1926, fared even worse when a pitching horse plunged two hoofs into a badger burrow and rolled with him.

"Broke my collarbone and three or four ribs," George recalled. "I didn't even saddle a horse for six weeks after that."

Even more menacing were prairie dog towns, which once dotted the Great Plains by the tens of thousands. Not only was a dog hole the perfect size to catch a drumming hoof, but the rodents also engineered upward-trending escape tunnels that undercut the surface and left it subject to collapse. Because prairie dogs could strip a range bare, cattlemen did everything possible to exterminate the mammals. Still, abandoned dog towns only increased a horseman's danger, for the holes grassed over and lay in wait to snare unsuspecting broncs.

Even with a respect for the hazards, a cowboy in prairie dog country was seldom master of his fate. Nineteen-year-old Aubrey Stokes, rustling horses in a Texas dog town at daybreak in 1926, broke his arm when his pony sprawled amid a storm of dust. That same year on a grassy lower Pecos mesa, Ollie Brown suffered a disfiguring injury in a similar wreck.

"He was running his pony as hard as he could," recalled Gid Reding, who witnessed Brown's mishap. "Ol' pony picked up a dog hole and Ollie slid out there a long ways and then turned over."

Reding immediately gigged his bronc and rushed to the cowhand's aid.

"When I got to him, he sat up and his lower lip was down under his chin," Reding recounted. "It was the danged-est lookin' thing, that ol' chin stickin' out there. I had to put my knee against his chest and pull it back."

A roper chasing a runaway on the Cross-B Ranch in Crosby County, Texas, in 1909. (E. E. Smith Collection, Nita Stewart Haley Memorial Library, Midland, Texas)

Brown recovered, but his lower lip would always bear the mark of his spill.

Less deforming but more serious was Walter Hoelscher's July 4, 1930, injury as he ran a herd of twenty to twenty-five calves across a Texas flat. "The horse hit a prairie dog hole and we started rolling," said Hoelscher. "It finally fell on me and I was knocked out."

When the waddy came to, he tried to mount his lame and bloody horse, only to find himself unable to swing his leg over. Gripping the underside of his knee, he dragged the limb across and fell forward over the saddle horn. Still, he had a job to do, and a cowboy wasn't one to shirk a duty. Forcing himself upright, Hoelscher finished penning the calves—even with injuries severe enough to require back surgery.

Hoelscher could have counted himself lucky; Bud Mayes remembered one dog hole victim who hovered between life and death for months before doctors released him from a West Texas hospital.

Even in an area free of animal burrows or other pitfalls, heavy rainfall could create hazards just as sinister. Otis Coggins, cutting cattle from a South Texas herd during a mid-1910s drizzle, broke his leg when his pony slipped down. His only doctor was a fellow waddy who immobilized the limb with boards and ducking.

Anytime runoff collected in pools, a horseman had to be especially vigilant, for footing was precarious in the underlying mud. Seventeen-year-old Si Loeffler recognized the danger as he wrangled horses on a dark Texas morning after a 1920 downpour, but he had limited options when his pony bolted with the remuda.

"I was seesawing him this way and that to keep him from getting too fast and getting in trouble," he remembered.

Too late, a flash of lightning revealed a water hole dead ahead.

"I tried to pull him around, but he hit that water and down he went," Loeffler narrated. "I was under him, laying in that mud and water."

Fearing that his foot might be lodged in the stirrup, Loeffler quickly seized the cheek of the hackamore to keep the horse from rising. It bought the young cowhand the time he needed to unbuckle the saddle by touch and free himself.

Like Loeffler, Thomas Henderson of Trans-Pecos Texas once found himself hung to a downed horse. The nineteen-year-old cowhand exhibited skill in clinging to a bronc pitching in a circle in 1927, but as he gigged the outlaw with big Chihuahua spurs, disaster erupted.

"I got my spur hung in that girt," Henderson related.

Powerless to quit the saddle, the cowboy could only steel himself as the horse fell broadside and pinned him.

"When he landed on that leg, I couldn't afford to let him get up, afraid he might stagger around and kick me a-loose and drag me to death," he remembered.

Calling upon all his horse savvy, Henderson clutched the saddle horn and held the animal in place. "You could hold a horse there forever—he can't do anything but pop his head on the ground," explained Henderson. Still, he needed the help of a passing cowboy to let the bronc make a controlled rise that freed him.

With skill and luck, Henderson and Loeffler had both escaped dire situations, but for other riders hung to a horse, the consequence could not have been more forbidding—dragged!

Hung to a Bronc

In them days a man had to be a man every day without no layoffs. Every day!

—Richard C. Phillips, cowhand

Mounting a skittish bronc in Texas in 1906 or 1907. (Photo by E. E. Smith, Library of Congress)

$\mathcal{W}$hen a cowhand dug his foot into a cowboy boot, he was not making a fashion statement. On the contrary, a boot was essential equipment that could spell the difference between life and death for a horseman. The pointed toe slipped easily into a stirrup, while the two-inch heel kept the foot firm against the stirrup bar. But the interaction of boot and stirrup could also make for trouble, especially with a spur jingling at a cowboy's heel.

"If that foot happened to slide through that stirrup and your horse throwed you, you was hung in your saddle," noted Joe Lambert, a cowboy of the 1910s.

In a split second of lost balance, it could happen—a boot driving through and locking, secured by spur and toe. If a rider went down in such a situation, he would be helpless as the horse kicked or whirled or bolted at breakneck speed. Short of rescue, a hung cowboy had only three decent chances.

His foot could dislodge by struggle or luck.

His boot could come off.

His spur strap could break.

There was also a fourth possibility, although no cowhand would have bet a plug nickle on it. In a last-ditch effort, a dragged rider might struggle for his pocketknife as he bounced like a rag doll. If he didn't uproot a stump or catch a crushing hoof or rock in the skull—and provided he could open and control the blade—he might succeed in cutting the stirrup leather.

Any way a cowhand looked at it, getting caught in the stirrup was like playing poker with the undertaker. Still, cowboys put themselves in jeopardy every time they stepped on, particularly if they faced broncs as snaky as the W outfit's remuda on the Pecos in 1895. One W cowhand, dragged as a consequence of trying to mount, seemed destined for a lonely grave.

"Instantly I saw the danger the waddy was in," recounted fellow cowhand William A. Preist. "I took aim with a rifle and shot the animal. The hoss tumbled to the ground. . . . The waddy untangled himself quickly and was none the worse for his experience."

On another Pecos country ranch in the late 1920s, Billy Rankin shared the W victim's distress. When Rankin roped a scampering heifer one day, the force ripped out the saddle horn and set the stage for calamity. Trying to mount up again later in the day, Rankin had to compensate for the missing horn. But broncs, like men, were creatures of habit, and the cowboy's unorthodox method spooked the horse.

"That SOB jumped and kicked me on the leg, and one foot hung in the stirrup," Rankin recounted. "It sure makes you have a lonesome feeling. He drug me about twenty-five feet and kicked me loose."

In dismounting, as well, a saddle horn played a pivotal safety role. In the late 1920s, West Texas cowboy Louis Baker watched a rider's hand slip from the horn as he started to step off. Suddenly the man's boot wedged in the stirrup, and had Baker not run up and seized the bronc, real tragedy could have followed.

"He said I saved his life," Baker remembered.

Paul Patterson, climbing off a small Indian horse on a West Texas ranch in the 1920s, had no rescuer as the animal wheeled with his foot in the stirrup. On the verge of bolting, the bronc abruptly fell, giving Patterson time to work his foot free.

"That was just an act of Providence," Patterson reflected.

Anytime a bronc went down, though, it was more likely to spawn trouble than alleviate it—an axiom to which L. Kinser could attest after a stirrup seized his boot in a 1920s horse fall. Shaken, the Texas cowhand lay helpless in a ditch as his bronc struggled up and threatened to run. To Kinser's amazement, however, the animal stood in place and allowed him to loosen the stirrup's clench.

"Don't think you don't thank Somebody upstairs for that," noted Kinser.

During the same era, Green Mankin faced an even worse predicament in a horse wreck in a Texas arroyo. As the bronc regained its feet and broke into a run, Mankin dangled backward from the animal's hips, the victim of a stirrup-hold on his boot. His spur dug fulcrum-like into the saddle seat, preventing him from turning over as he flopped with the bronc's every kick. He seemed powerless, but he kept up the fight and finally tumbled free with another tale of narrow escape to relate.

"I been in the worst places you ever saw—looked like there wasn't no chance to get out of 'em," Mankin observed in the twilight of a long life.

For some horse wreck victims, however, the grip of a stirrup meant serious injury or death, even with heroic efforts by others to stave off catastrophe. Bill Shields, cowboying in eastern New Mexico in 1928, called upon all his skills to aid one cowhand who jammed a foot in a stirrup in a horse fall.

"The horse went to runnin' and drug him right down the fence fifty or sixty feet," Shields recounted. "I had to ride up on the side the boy was dragging on. That boogered my horse, and it was hard to get to him. I was reaching out, getting hold of the reins, when his horse kicked him and broke his neck."

In a horse wreck in Motley County, Texas, in the 1960s, a cowhand paid the ultimate price for hanging in a stirrup. "I saw the horse draggin' him," remembered Jones Taylor, a cowboy from the 1920s on. "The horse didn't go very far, but it killed him."

The worst perpetrator of a stirrup-hold was a cloud-jumping bronc that could cost a cowboy his equilibrium in an instant. If a boot thrust through a flying stirrup, a rider faced his greatest test—stay put and live, or fall and maybe die.

"He got me overbalanced and I never could straighten back up," said Ted Laughlin of one New Mexico bronc in the early 1930s. "The pony throwed me off and hung me in the stirrup. He was going in a circle and I was swinging out from him. The spur leather broke and I come loose, or he could've kicked me to death."

Slim Armentrout, likewise snared in the 1920s, endured an extended ordeal as his horse dragged him two hundred yards in a dead run across a mesquite valley. "I didn't have much time to think—I was trying to get loose," recalled the West Texas cowboy. "Finally my boot come off."

Sometimes, a dollar-a-day cowhand's financial standing forced him to wear lace-up boots, which only served to increase the peril. This was especially true of weekend cowboys, men from other trades who occasionally worked on ranches. Billy Rankin, a hand on the Foy Proctor spread in Texas, recalled a moonlighting barber who lodged a lace-up boot in the stirrup in 1924. "That horse drug him twenty-five or thirty feet, just a-bouncin' like a rag," recounted Rankin.

When the man rolled free, Rankin rushed to his side. "That scared the hell out of me!" exclaimed Rankin.

"Aw," said the barber, "I was gonna get out of it all right—I was fixin' to unlace that boot."

It was the kind of confidence that every cowboy needed in dealing with an intimidating bronc. Still, the quickest way for a rider to get in trouble was to take undue pride in his ability—the very mistake that almost killed Charles K. Smith of West Texas soon after the Great War.

"I was always wanting to try myself out," Smith remembered. "Cowboys had a way that made some horses buck—just run your thumbs up their neck while they're lopin' along."

When Smith did exactly that on this day, his pony gave him more than he bargained for and threw him. The cowhand hit the ground but couldn't escape the stirrup, and an instant later he was plowing

Edwin Sanders saddling a troublesome bronc on the ED Ranch near Crowell, Texas, in 1906. (Photo by E. E. Smith, Library of Congress)

the desert floor at reckless speed. The dust rose in a plume, choking him, and he could feel the very wind of those pummeling hoofs. Finally, his boot came off, saving his life.

"I was a fool," Smith reflected in 1990 with the wisdom of ninety-five years.

Sometimes, desperation could drive a cowhand to a feat of skill that defied all odds. A case in point involved Orval Sparks, who, at six feet, two and a half inches, was long-legged for a waddy, necessitating that his stirrups ride low. Cowboying alone in West Texas sheep country about 1940, Sparks was caught off guard when his horse downed its head and kicked to the sky. His foot drove through the stirrup as he tumbled off, binding him to an animal that hurtled across the pasture like a runaway train.

"He was headed for some awful thick brush and rocks and I was jumpin' up and down," Sparks recounted. "I always carried a sharp pocketknife—I realized it was right then or never."

Fighting for the blade and flipping it open, Sparks lunged for the low-hanging stirrup leather and began to slash. The bronc dragged him fifty yards before he severed it, freeing himself just before a rock or stump might have sealed his doom.

"You can do a lot when your life depends on it," Sparks observed fifty years later.

As Sparks proved, the chances of surviving a dragging might depend on a cowhand's wherewithal to respond coolly in a critical moment. But displaying a fighting spirit for a few heart-pounding seconds was one thing; doing so throughout an hours-long nightmare would have tested the mettle of even the most experienced cowhand. Yet, it was a ten-year-old cowboy who set standards for courage and indomitable will in a dragging incident on a Texas ranch about 1915.

Riding the pasture with his young brother and sister, A. W. Hoelscher toppled from the saddle and plunged a foot through the stirrup. As his horse exploded into a gallop, his siblings gigged their animals and gave chase. Soon, a frightening pattern emerged— A. W.'s bronc would come to a standstill, only to bolt and drag him farther whenever either of them neared. Death seemed almost certain as the ordeal lingered for thirty minutes . . . an hour . . . two hours. Finally, his siblings managed to pen the horse, allowing them to rescue the still-conscious boy.

Avoiding a stirrup disaster wasn't always possible, but a rider could at least hope for the best and keep the saddle girded tightly. The consequences of not doing so could be deadly.

Pulling rein at rimrock falling away in mountainous West Texas country in 1917, several cowhands dismounted and secured their cinches. The trail below was treacherous, and prudence dictated that they take every precaution. Only Charlie Lyons, astride an

Zack T. Burkett of the LS Ranch in Texas descending a perilous slope before 1911. (E. E. Smith Collection, Nita Stewart Haley Memorial Library, Midland, Texas)

ebony horse known as the Four-Time Black, elected to forgo the procedure—a decision that cost him his life. As his pony negotiated the steep slope, the stirrup turned with the saddle and clutched the falling cowboy's boot. The Four-Time Black, spooked by its shifting burden, jumped into a run and dragged Lyons to death.

The threat from a slipping saddle was not limited to a stirrup-hold, for the horn could seize just as assuredly. In brushy country near Fluvanna, Texas, about 1926, Bill Townsend urged his horse into a lope, unaware that the cinch was loose. As he leaned to dodge a limb, the saddle suddenly rolled with him. He bounced on the ground but couldn't free himself from the boogered horse—the saddle horn had hooked his legging.

"He drug me a hundred and fifty yards, just a-kickin' and a-buckin' all over me," Townsend recounted. "I was holdin' the reins, tryin' to pull up on 'em, but I really didn't know what I was doin'. Finally it tore my legging off, and that turned him loose."

A saddle horn could plague a cowboy in other ways as well. Frank Derrick of the Texas Panhandle once buckled a figure eight hobble around his waist, only to have it slip over the horn when his horse broke in two.

"It felt like having a seat belt," he remembered.

Imperiled, Derrick worked feverishly to extricate himself as he clung to the pigeon-winging bronc. "When you get in a tight [fix] like that, you've got more than two hands," he observed decades later.

After a harried minute, Derrick finally worked the hobble free, a little wiser for his close shave.

Extraneous objects on a cowboy's person or saddle were always a threat to snare a rider, but it often took a freak accident to convince a young waddy. On a chilly Texas morning about 1917, Bud Mayes buttoned his coat and forked a black horse with a reputation for being "tolerable mean." When the warming sun rose higher, the teenager removed his coat and tied it to the cantle of his saddle. As he spurred his mount after a cow in a pitted arroyo, the black horse stumbled in a hole and fell.

"My spur hung in this coat," recounted Mayes. "He drug me about fifteen feet, kicked me a time or two. I thought, 'Well, you've killed me.' And the spur leather broke and I fell off."

A spur could also lodge in the flank cinch, a development just as ripe for tragedy. Shorty Northcutt once found himself in just such a predicament astride an outlaw horse on the Spade outfit in Texas.

"He was just a-pitchin' and a-havin' a fit, nearly comin' over backwards," he recounted.

Knowing he had no other choice, Northcutt made the ride of his life, buying enough time for another cowhand to grab the bronc and save him.

"That horse would've had to pull my arm off to have got rid of me," Northcutt later reflected.

Bill Shields, in similar jeopardy after a 1927 horse wreck on an eastern New Mexico ranch, was also the beneficiary of a rescue. Thrown but pinned to the cinch, the stunned cowhand clung by instinct to a slicker at his cantle as the bronc ran.

"I wasn't a-draggin' on the ground; I was just hangin' back in his flanks," Shields related. "There happened to be a couple of boys with me, and they caught him."

Of all the ways a cowboy might hang to a horse, the most dangerous may have been by lariat. A twentieth-century cowhand generally used a thirty- to thirty-five-foot rope, three strands of grass strong enough to upend a sprinting calf. He carried it coiled and attached by string to the saddle, a location that gave him quick access as he readied to drop a loop. No threat to break, a lariat could catch a falling cowboy's spur in its coil, or his arm or leg somewhere in its length.

Among the unfortunate was twelve-year-old Douglas Poage, the victim of a late-1910s prank in which another cowhand poked his horse under the tail and made it pitch. As Poage tumbled off, his spur hooked the coil of his rope. Under the force, the lariat played out and held fast as he struck the ground.

"That horse took off with me sitting down at the end of that rope," narrated Poage. "He drug me about four hundred yards—I didn't know what to think."

Poage frantically searched for his pocketknife, but the blade had already spilled from his trousers. Meanwhile, his fellow rider was in hot pursuit, doing his utmost to catch the runaway bronc.

"He was about even with me when my spur come off over my heel," remembered Poage, who sustained only abrasions.

In a similar accident in the early 1930s, twelve-year-old Joe Thomas Davidson narrowly avoided death in rimrock country in West Texas. When his Shetland bucked him off, the young cowboy hung a spur in his coiled rope. As in Poage's mishap, the lariat kept its hold even as Davidson slammed to the turf.

"That horse was draggin' him, runnin' full speed and headed for the rimrocks," recalled Ted Powers, who immediately gave chase.

As the Shetland veered to avoid a five-foot stand of prickly pear, momentum rolled Davidson and snapped his spur strap. He plunged into the thorns' heart but nevertheless escaped lucky—twenty feet down the Shetland's path lay boulders ready to crush.

On occasion, the fight-or-flee instinct of a cowhand dragged at rope's end could inspire him to unyielding determination. No cowboy ever displayed such better than Alf Tollett, an old-time Texas rider who tangled a foot in his lariat when his horse fell. As the bronc rose and started to run, Tollett sat back on the rope and threw the horse—then threw the animal a second time to give himself a chance to lunge for the saddle and leap on. Only after he was safely astride did he manage to free his boot.

A rider's arm and wrist were also prime candidates to get caught in a rope, especially if he fell from the saddle with coil in hand. All that likely spared Spade waddy Ralph Carter an early grave after such a mishap was an exhausted horse. As he tried to rope a coyote on a cold West Texas morning in the 1930s, his dun bronc fell, and the lariat wrapped around his upper arm. The dun dragged the lone cowhand a bruising quarter-mile that peeled the skin from his face and shredded his sheepskin coat.

The toll was far greater on Owen Lockler and Lester "Gabe" Beauchamp, West Texas cowboys who died in separate rope-related draggings in the 1920s or 1930s. No one ever knew the exact sequence of events, but when searchers located their respective bodies, Beauchamp's arm bore a rope burn, while Lockler's wrist was still bound to his horse. The latter man's body, dragged throughout a rainy night, was particularly disturbing, for the miles had stripped every stitch of clothing.

Such a memory could haunt even the most stoic cowhand.

"That's the most horrible thing that you ever saw," observed

Frank Yeary, who lost a friend in a 1940s dragging on the Four Sixes in the Texas Panhandle. "[My friend's] horse either throwed him or he fell, and he got tangled up in his rope. His horse drug him four miles through that brush and them rocks."

Tom Blasingame had two sets of horrid memories to suppress—a dragging death in Arizona before 1934 and a similar tragedy in Briscoe County, Texas, in the early 1950s. The Briscoe accident was especially troubling, for Blasingame came frustratingly close to saving the fourteen-year-old cowhand.

"We jumped a bunch of wild cattle, and all of us got ahead of this kid," Blasingame recalled. "He wasn't supposed to take his rope down, but I guess he did. Directly, my son hollered—I looked back and here come that boy's horse draggin' him through them mesquites and rocks."

Wheeling his animal, Blasingame tried to head off the runaway, but the boy's horse dodged and fled at a full gallop.

"We finally roped the horse and stopped him, but that boy was broke all to pieces, just limber as a rag," Blasingame remembered.

A fatality stemming from a dragging always had a powerful impact, but never more so than on J. P. Benard, an impressionable eight-year-old on a Brazos country ranch in Texas. In the late 1870s and early 1880s, the boy learned cow work at the feet of a cowboy named Gable, a seasoned hand with a mysterious past.

"Old Gable was better to me than my own parents and acted like a dad to me," Benard reflected at age sixty-five.

Gable introduced little J. P. to roping, although the boy's father refused to let him practice on animals of size. The elder Benard's caution was well-founded, for in 1881 Gable met with a deadly accident upon roping a yearling. As the loop settled over the sprinting beef, Gable's horse should have pegged—dug in to absorb the force of lariat snapping taut. Instead, the bronc reared, driving Gable's foot through the stirrup and throwing him off into a stump.

The horse took flight, dragging him around a clump of cedars, and even though another rider saved him from immediate death, Gable's fate was sealed—a broken rib had punctured his heart.

"We buried him in our front yard, alongside my granddad," said Benard. "We had to, because we didn't know where to send his body. He never got no mail, never went to town, was always out of sight when strangers came to the place, and never told anything about his past life."

At least they had spared a caring cowhand a forgotten grave, but the potential for a lonely three-by-six resting place would persist for generations of ropers to come.

Lariats and Devil Horns

We had to take the risks though, because [a man] either worked cattle in those days, or he didn't work.

—J. C. Hess, cowhand

Tom Blasingame roping a calf on the Matador Ranch in Texas in the 1920s. (J. Evetts Haley Collection, Nita Stewart Haley Memorial Library, Midland, Texas)

A horseman had many reasons for roping an animal, all of them involving control. Perhaps he needed to doctor a wormy cow or drag a calf to the branding fire. Maybe a couple of bulls clashed at a water hole, or a steer proved too ornery for driving. Unusual circumstances sometimes created a necessity that no cowhand could anticipate; in 1893, Julius Henderson had to rope and drag fifty cattle across a West Texas railroad when the leery beeves refused to cross on their own.

A lariat was a thirty-five-foot extension of the man-horse composite that was a cowboy, but it could also be a deadly foil, linking as it did powerful brutes that acted in opposition to one another. As a bolting steer struck the end of a catch rope and a thousand-pound horse braced for impact, the fireworks could resemble an irresistible force meeting an immovable object. One thing was certain—tragedy awaited any rider unlucky enough to get caught between.

Risk, however, was part of a cowboy's life, and he couldn't afford to be intimidated as he leaned to the side of a galloping bronc to cast a rattler-strike loop. Even so, plenty could go wrong from the moment he twirled a lariat over his Stetson.

When Green Mankin jerked his coil from his saddle and prepared to rope a Brahma heifer in Trans-Pecos Texas in the 1920s, he failed to reckon with the gusting wind. "I built me a loop and made a run at her to rope her," he narrated. "The rope blowed around, and that big loop got under my ol' horse's tail. He hung his head, and I tell you, I didn't pull any leather because I couldn't find any."

As the horse pitched wildly, all Mankin could do was try to anticipate. "My knees was way up over the saddle, and I was just tryin' to be where he was gonna hit the ground the next time," he recalled. "I thought he was gonna lose me in spite. But by golly, I rode him until he finally just pulled up his head."

A roper also couldn't permit his loop to interfere with another rider's horse. In a box canyon south of Santa Fe, New Mexico, in 1963, Douglas Poage brought his pony abreast of a running steer to keep it from veering into brush, thus giving another cowhand a chance to lasso the animal.

"When he roped the steer, the loop came around and forefooted my horse," recounted Poage. "We was runnin' just about as fast as we could run, and we really rolled."

Even if a cowboy watched from the sidelines, a stray loop could inflict pain and disfigurement. Marvin Hooper, afoot in a West Texas corral in the 1930s, suffered a broken nose when another cowhand's lariat slipped off a colt and came flying.

"My nose laid over, and I could see the darned thing with the corner of my eye," remembered Hooper.

To tighten a lariat against saddle in the heat of action, a cowboy from northern or west coast ranges would "dally," a corruption of the Spanish term *dar la vuelta*, or "give a turn." As a roper dropped a loop over the head of a barreling steer, he quickly wrapped his end of the lariat around the saddle horn two or three times. When the line pulled taut, slippage and friction helped absorb the impact. Although dallying had advantages—a horse maintained better balance, and a rider could free the rope in an emergency—the frenzied maneuver could catch a finger or thumb between lariat and saddle horn.

"We called that 'dally, then tally'—see if you've got all your fingers left," 1920s cowhand Paul Patterson observed wryly.

Indeed, in the 1930s, Montana and Wyoming were full of cowboys with missing thumbs and fingers. Even if an old cowhand retained his digits, he likely exhibited the marks of a hard life before the lariat.

"Both my hands are crippled—got jerked and burned with ropes branding big cattle on foot," seventy-one-year-old Teddy Blue Abbott wrote from Gilt Edge, Montana, in 1931.

Dallying demanded not only dexterity in a rider, but expertise in commanding a horse while controlling a lariat's slippage about the horn. Fish Wilson, dallying after roping a horse in the Texas Panhandle, was caught unawares as his animal buried its head between its knees. "He jerked them reins through my hand and blowed up with me," he remembered. "He threwed me up and I turned over and come down flat on my back."

Until rodeos popularized dallying, a Texas cowpoke usually kept the end of his lariat tied "hard and fast" to the saddle horn with a figure eight knot, thereby trusting his horse to withstand the full brunt of a fleeing animal's power. "It didn't matter whether they were roping an elephant or a jackrabbit, Texas cowboys let the horse take care of it," said Patterson.

On occasion, however, a bronc was not equal to the task. In West Texas in 1917, fifteen-year-old Alphonzo Dunnahoo fractured his hip when an ornery cow at lariat's end jerked his horse down. Under similar circumstances in 1927, a burro felled John Patterson's bronc and broke the Texas cowhand's leg so severely that he was unable even to sit for six weeks.

Accidents, it seemed, loomed at every throw of a loop. Irvin Cumbie, roping on a Texas ranch in the early 1900s, got his hand snared in the lariat between saddle horn and wild cow. "The cow didn't get away," Cumbie noted with typical cowhand pride, "but I almost lost a hand then and there."

Despite his immediate reprieve, Cumbie remained under the threat of amputation throughout several weeks in a hospital.

In 1935, a similar accident maimed twenty-three-year-old Shorty Northcutt, whose horse broke in two when he roped a buck sheep on the Spade Ranch in Texas.

"It'd been a-rainin' and my rope was real limber," Northcutt recounted at age seventy-seven. "When I changed hands, it drawed up on two fingers and jerked them off. . . . I had to learn to rope all over again."

Even if a cowpuncher eluded injury as a lariat brought a fugitive animal to a standstill, the taut line could prove treacherous. Bud Mayes's horse once stepped across the lariat in such a circumstance, forcing him to brace for a frightful wreck. Fortunately, the horse held its ground, but one dun bronc in the early 1940s made fellow Texas cowhand Tom Parisher reconsider the wisdom of tying hard and fast.

"When a cow would hit the end of the rope, that horse would go to pitching around and around, tanglin' you up," he recalled. "I never would tie on him anymore—I'd just *dar la vuelta.*"

On a West Texas ranch in the 1930s, Walton Poage watched a spinning horse wrap a roper in a stretched lariat and drag him from

OR rider Jim Harmon with a roped yearling on the Arizona range in 1909. (E. E. Smith Collection, Nita Stewart Haley Memorial Library, Midland, Texas)

the saddle. Caught between bronc and lassoed cow, the cowhand seemed headed for the eternal range until Poage and other onlookers rushed in and grabbed the horse. Their quick reaction spared the cowhand, but Green Mankin had no rescuers in a similar incident in the region.

Riding a greenbroke bronc, Mankin came upon a screwworm-infested bull and decided to doctor it. Just as he roped the animal, his horse began to whirl.

"The first thing I knew, the rope was around me," he remembered. "If that ol' bull had started to run, it'd've been *adios, Jesus.* I worked and eased that horse around and finally got enough slack to get loose."

Safety wasn't assured even if a horse cooperated from the start, for a lassoed animal could deliver trouble of its own. A cow might turn with flashing horns and disembowel a roper's bronc, a situation that once forced Walter Boren to destroy a horse on the OS Ranch in Texas. Orval Sparks, facing similar menace on the Spade outfit about 1948, had no choice but to reach for his pocketknife.

"That outlaw cow was chasing me and hooking my horse, and I couldn't get loose from her," remembered Sparks, whose lariat was tied to the saddle horn. "I had to cut my rope to get away."

Another set of angry horns spawned a harrowing moment for a Sugg Ranch cowboy along the Middle Concho River in Texas. To gain maximum control over a rebellious bull, Brook Campbell and a second rider took up lariats. Campbell successfully roped the brute's head, but his partner's loop went astray and caught fast around the swishing tail.

"[I] hollered at the boy that if my rope broke, he would certainly have the bull by the tail," Campbell recounted.

Seconds later, Campbell's lariat indeed snapped, leaving his partner vulnerable as the bull spun and charged. The impact dropped the cowhand's horse and severed the cinch, and when the bull proceeded to bolt for the "high lonesome," the saddle went with it at rope's end.

"Three of us boys were after him by this time, and across the creek he went," narrated Campbell. "Just as we crossed, one of the boys made a grab at the saddle, wrapped it around a tree, and that jerked the old bull's tail off. That fellow was known as the Bobtail Bull forever afterwards."

Although such incidents could provide fodder for cow-camp humor, tragedy was just as likely to result. Champion roper Jake McClure, putting his string on a calf on a southeastern New Mexico ranch about 1940, never expected the beef to wheel and pile into the bronc's neck. The horse fell, crushing McClure's chest under the cantle of the saddle. Eleven days later, the cowboy died in a nearby hospital.

Anytime a roper threw a wormy bovine and dismounted to apply medicine, speed and technique were all-important in avoiding injury. Jumping on the tripped animal, the cowhand would hold it down by planting a boot in the neck and immobilizing its forelegs with his body. The real challenge would come after he tended the sores, for as soon as he slipped the rope free and backed away, the beef might jump up fighting.

On the Tankersley Ranch in Texas, J. H. Yardley once went down under the charge of a wormy bull he had loosed. Desperate, he crawled for the security of a clump of bushes, where he lay half-stunned as the enraged animal snorted and slung dirt. Suddenly the fiend "roared out a big bellow" and breached Yardley's refuge as limbs splintered and flew.

"As he would horn down at me, I would dig him in the eyes with my thumbs," remembered Yardley. "That slowed him down a little, but not enough to keep him from ramming his horn in my side, lifting me clear of the brush, and tossing me about ten feet over the brush pile."

Cross-B cowhand Frank Smith planting his boot on a roped maverick in Crosby County, Texas, about 1909. (E. E. Smith Collection, Nita Stewart Haley Memorial Library, Midland, Texas)

Bloody and weak, Yardley could only flatten himself and feign death.

"He rushed after me, but . . . only nosed and sniffed over my body and walked away, slobbering like a mad dog," related the cowhand. "That was one of my narrowest escapes."

Anytime a waddy doctored and released a longhorn, the danger heightened, for the only safety lay in a quick getaway by pony.

"[Longhorns] seldom failed to make a run at your horse," M. H. Loy noted in 1930. "I saw an old cow catch a horse at the lower end of the shoulder and cut a gash about four inches long. The horse was slow about starting."

Devil horns demanded a cowhand's vigilance even if no lariat was involved, for range cattle of any breed could be wild and bad-tempered. "If you didn't have one charge you—boy, you wasn't around much cows," observed Fish Wilson of the Texas Panhandle. Before a troublesome bovine got out of control, a cowpoke might spit tobacco juice in its eyes and half blind it. If caught afoot in a threatening situation, a cowboy might sidestep an attack like a bullfighter or roll forward into a charge and force the beef to hurdle his body. The latter maneuver was risky, for not only could a flinty hoof crush him, the bovine might halt and start rooting with deadly horns.

On the Muleshoe Ranch in Texas, George Black once ran in front of a rampaging bull to distract it from a would-be victim. The tactic worked, but the widow-maker proceeded to turn its horns on Black, who threw himself into a roll straight for the drumming hoofs. He expected the bull to jump him, but instead he came face to face with a pawing demon intent on goring.

"Quicker'n the eye could follow the move, he jerked his six-shooter out and pumped five shots in that bull's belly," recounted Black's nephew, W. L. Dobbs, who witnessed the incident. "The bull sorta shook his head, walked to his left for about ten feet, then dropped over dead."

Some cowhands kept a revolver close for the very purpose of shooting an attacking bovine. Tom Mills, tallying livestock in a Rio Grande pen in 1880, started to a sudden "Look out!" and found a bull bearing down on him. He lunged for a six-shooter dangling from his saddle horn and spun with a finger on the trigger.

"I hit him a lucky shot, and he was comin' with such force, he fell with his head right at my feet," Mills remembered.

Even hugging a saddle didn't guarantee a horseman safety, although his elevated position limited a beef's attack to leg or bronc. But a rider and his mount might avoid a ripping horn only to face equally grave injury before the muscled beef's immense power. On Salt Creek in Texas, Bob Pierce almost died when a ferocious bull plowed under his bronc, lifted the animal's hind legs, and somersaulted the horse.

At times, a bovine could become so crazed that it would even challenge an automobile. As Walter Hoelscher drove a dozen cattle down a dirt road in West Texas in 1925, a cow brushed an adjacent barbed wire fence. Bloodied, the animal flew into a rage and vented its wrath on anything that moved—including a passing auto.

"She tried to get the driver but missed that man and bent the car in," remembered Hoelscher.

About 1912, Charles K. Smith of the Davis Mountains of Texas tangled with a horned terror that had an equal dislike for autos.

"Of all the cattle I ever handled, he was the meanest, wildest, craziest," Smith reflected at age ninety-five. "We called him Pancho Villa. He wasn't that overly big, but gosh, he was bravo. He could jump an ordinary wire fence like it wasn't there."

Part of a string of Mexican steers imported by rail, Pancho Villa was an unknown commodity as cowpokes unloaded the cattle cars and started the herd for the Bill Jones ranch. For mile after weary mile, the tired steer plodded along with the drags, doing little to raise Smith's eyebrows. But that all changed when a dust plume signaled the approach of an auto driven by a woman.

"He charged that automobile and broke a light," Smith related. "Only time I ever saw that in my life."

Rounding up Pancho Villa one fall, Smith and George Jones had to employ a bait-and-lure method. After both had roped the outlaw, the cowhands took respective positions front and rear.

"We'd let him run at the one in front and try to hook his horse, and when he got too close, we'd stop and hold him," Smith recounted. "We were probably a mile from the pen, about three o'clock one afternoon. It was dark when we got him to the pen."

One of the most volatile situations on the range involved a bull or steer fight, yet a cowboy often put himself in harm's way for either practical or entertainment purposes. With horns clashing and hoofs churning, the powerful beasts would bloody the turf amid

A cowboy pausing to watch bulls spar on the LS Ranch in Texas in 1907. (E. E. Smith Collection, Nita Stewart Haley Memorial Library, Midland, Texas)

snorts that were sure to lure any nearby rider. Even if he chose not to separate the animals, a cowpuncher might hold his horse and watch the action through the stirring alkali—a decision that could make him as much a participant as a spectator.

On the Kyle spread along the Pecos in the early 1920s, Bill Eddins pulled rein at a windmill to watch bulls battle for dominance. Despite his bronc's reputation for throwing riders, Eddins remained confident; he believed he had already taken the bucking animal's best in an earlier episode. Now, though, as he took his bronc closer, a bull broke from the melee and charged, suddenly elevating the pony's sky-flying abilities.

"That horse started to get away from there, and just as that bull went behind that horse, he broke in two with me," recalled Eddins. "I guarantee you, he pitched that time—I got both spurs pulled off."

Eddins was lucky to stay astride and withdraw to safety, but if a rider found retreat impractical, his life might hinge on the kind of quick thinking and improvisation that Alton Davis once displayed in the Texas Hill Country. As the YO horseman worked cattle in a sprawling pen that encompassed big mesquites, he became trapped between fighting steers. When the bovines turned their wicked horns on him, Davis ran his horse under a mesquite and swung up into the branches. Secure in his perch, he watched the steers mill angrily just below.

"They didn't bother my horse; he just stood there, and they'd run up close and turn," Davis remembered. "They was after *me*, was what they was after."

Sundown exacerbated the dangers of a bull fight, for nightfall limited a cowboy's vision but had little effect on cattle. Even if a rider could hear the bellowing of fighting bulls, as Thomas Henderson could as he rode up to a Chihuahuan Desert water hole on a black night in the early 1900s, he was unlikely to pinpoint the brutes. In the crash of bodies and thunder of hoofs, however, Henderson surmised the story of a vanquished animal taking flight.

"I didn't know where he was going, and I didn't move," remembered the Texas cowhand. "I thought, 'Well, hell, maybe he'll miss me.' But he didn't. He just sideswiped my horse and staggered him."

Night or day, it was seldom a pretty picture if a bull broke from a fight and squarely rammed a cowboy's bronc. On the Middle Concho in Texas, Buck Porter escaped death by a mere thread in such a collision.

"Buck was sitting sidewise on his horse, and it looked like he went about ten feet high," related W. J. D. Carr, who had joined Porter to watch the skirmishing bulls. "As he came down right on the old bull's horns, he was grazed clear around the stomach."

Watching a battle was dangerous enough, but breaking up a pair of rampaging bulls took reckless abandon. When two of these enormous animals once sparred on a Texas roundup, the owner rushed in on horseback and poked the stronger with a pole.

"[The bull] whirled and made a rush for the horse, struck him just behind the shoulder, and killed him instantly," remembered J. F. Henderson, a witness to the incident.

The rider leaped from the falling saddle and scrambled away, narrowly avoiding a crazed beast that gored the dead horse again and again.

The close quarters of a pen could make for an especially perilous situation with evil-eyed cattle, for trouble could erupt in an instant, and opportunity for escape was limited. Even an animal as seemingly innocuous as a milk cow might give a cowboy more than he could handle.

When youngster Paul Patterson once sauntered across a Texas corral attached to a barn, a milk cow interpreted the boy's approach as a threat to her calf and charged. Suddenly, the cow's curving horns pinned him flush against the barn.

"She was pushin' like everything, but she didn't even touch me 'cause I was in between her horns," Patterson remembered. "If I'd've been a little bigger and her horns had been a different shape, she'd've mashed the heck out of me."

About 1930, a motley-faced steer's unusual horns offered no asylum to an L7 cowhand in a railroad stock pen near Odessa, Texas. Upon shipping this steer and three thousand others from El Paso, ranch manager W. W. "Billy" Brunson had wired his son his concerns:

"Watch the motley-faced steer with the stub horn—he's dangerous."

Nevertheless, as L7 cowboys unloaded rail car after rail car, the elder Brunson's warning served only to confuse; every car had multiple animals that fit the description. Finally, a motley-faced steer spilled out and eyed the punchers with the demeanor of a fighting bull. Singling out a cowhand afoot in the water lot, the steer descended on him with malevolent intent. The cowpoke fled, slinging turf with boots that weren't meant for walking, and hurdled a water trough a scant step ahead of the fiend. Fanned by those terrible horns, the man lunged for a fence beyond and began scrambling up. Even so, he would have caught a horn in the britches if the steer hadn't stumbled in the trough and fallen.

"Well," opined Brunson's son, who had watched the frantic race, "that must've been the one Daddy was talkin' about."

If a cowpoke straddled a bronc in such a situation, he might urge it toward the fence and hope for the best. Texas cowpoke J. F. Henderson, afoot in a long-ago branding pen, angered a big bull and sprang on his horse. When a ripping horn grazed his leg, he touched spurs to the bronc and made it jump the fence.

"That was all that saved us both," Henderson later reflected.

No matter if a bovine was bull or heifer, horned or polled, a cowhand had to respect its ability to incur injury. Otherwise, he might meet the fate of a squint-eyed old cowboy who had just helped brand a one-eyed JA heifer in a Texas corral in 1941. When Fish Wilson and another waddy tried to turn the heifer out the gate, the animal grew belligerent and twice ran them up the fence.

"The old man was just standin' out there laughin' in the middle of the lot, but I didn't think it was so funny," related Wilson. "He was laughin' so loud I guess she heard him."

Wheeling, the heifer charged the cowhand, who took flight too late. "She knocked that old man down, his feet went up, and he come down and just lay there," remembered Wilson.

Rushing to his aid, Wilson and other cowhands roused the stunned victim with a bucket of water. "Are you hurt, Dad? Are you, hurt?" pressed the old cowpoke's anxious son.

"Son," he managed, "I'm hurt, and hurt bad."

Hospitalized, the veteran cowpuncher had planted his boot in a JA stirrup for the last time.

Regardless of whether a bovine faced gate or chute, dipping vat or trailer, the brute sometimes just had a mind of its own, with perilous consequences to a cowhand. As a rider tried to pen a stubborn cow, for example, a horn might brand his leg or bloody his horse. In one such incident at a corral gate near Elida, New Mexico, about 1926, Ted Laughlin watched a cow plunge a fatal horn into a fellow horseman's bronc.

One of the most treacherous spots for a cowboy was inside a crowding pen, which restricted him to foot as he chided a bovine toward a chute. Even with gentle cattle, patience was essential, but cowhands sometimes had little forbearance out of the saddle. George Teague of Texas, in a crowding pen with a bull one day, grew frustrated when the normally docile animal resisted a congested chute. When Teague began whipping the bull with the double of a rope, the bovine went berserk and drove him up a fence. A second man, Bill Boyd, wasn't as elusive and took a brutal horn in the hip before reaching safety.

In another crowding pen incident, Texas cowboy Bud Mayes suffered greater injury when a two-year-old bull refused to enter a chute. "He'd start in and come back, and he'd always hook at me or kick at me as he passed on by," remembered Mayes.

The determined cowpuncher redoubled his efforts, only to find himself between fierce horns and retreating frantically. Trapped against a big stump in midpen, the cowhand yelled for help as he wrestled those hooking horns and took a battering.

"Finally, the bull backed off and I grabbed the gate," continued Mayes. "When I did, the bull hooked his horns under the gate and pulled it off the hinges, and me and the gate both went down."

Rescued by a Mexican cowboy wielding an iron rod, Mayes spent several days nursing abrasions and bruises in a hospital.

Urging a beef into a dipping vat was no less challenging. On the Schreiner and Halff Ranch in South Texas one night in the 1920s, Otis Coggins forked a bronc to help dip hundreds of three- and four-year-old Brahma-mix steers. In all the shadowy stirring, Coggins never realized that a big steer had gored his horse, but when the bronc began to nicker and stumble, he knew something was wrong.

"I could feel somethin' cold on my leg and on my foot in the stirrup," related the cowpoke, who immediately reined the animal into the open. "I found blood all over my leggings and boot. I rode the ol' pony out about ten or fifteen feet and he fell dead. That horn went clear through into his heart."

When trailers were introduced to the range, a waddy had yet another risky situation with which to cope. Ted Powers, a septuagenarian in the early 1980s, sustained a permanent knot on his rib cage when a heifer resisted loading in Coryell County, Texas. Another elderly cowboy, Vance Davis, suffered a severe neck injury trying to load a Hereford bull on a spread elsewhere in Texas in the late 1970s. Standing in a corral as a trailer backed into position, Davis made the mistake of taking his eyes off the horned brute.

"Just as I heard him snuff, he hit me," Davis recalled. "He picked me up and threw me up in the air three times before he quit. He sure was a-handlin' me rough."

The actions of a domesticated animal were at least predictable, however, while those of wild beasts and slithering devils could imperil even the wariest cowhand.

Claw and Fang

The old days on the range were the best I ever had.

—P. L. Cowan, cowhand

A cowhand watches over the remuda. (Photo by E. E. Smith, Library of Congress)

When a cowhand took a seat in the saddle and put a hand on the horn, he usually fancied himself "the best damned cowboy ever was born," as one old song has it. What he lacked in confidence, he made up in bravado, especially around greenhorns. To hear him tell it, he could rope and ride anything with hair on it, be it mustang or grizzly or some fork-tailed creature yet unnamed.

The truth was, however, that a wildlife encounter could set him longing to face nothing more exotic than a snaky bronc or demon-eyed bull. The latter creatures he might never master but at least could understand, while the ways of wild animals were beyond his ken and thus fraught with danger.

When C. E. Settler heard a low rumbling beyond a rise as he rode across West Texas in the 1870s, he initially mistook it for innocent thunder. As the seconds ticked by, however, the sound not only persisted, but intensified until the very ground shook. Suddenly, stampeding buffalo burst into view, an unstoppable black tide sweeping straight toward him.

He wheeled his mare and fled, but a gopher hole snapped the horse's leg and sent Settler tumbling across the prairie. When he looked up, he found the mare wallowing on the ground and the rampaging buffalo almost upon him. Lunging for the saddle scabbard, he jerked out a Winchester carbine and pumped shot after shot into the oncoming leaders. Buffalo fell, one after the other, the carcasses piling before him and forming a barricade that forced succeeding animals to storm past left or right. He huddled there for minutes or hours, enduring an earthquake and choking on the hanging dust as thousands of buffalo hurdled by.

Buffalo soon became such a novelty, however, that a cowboy might seize every opportunity to test his roping skills on one. "The worst mess I ever got into roping wild animals was roping a two-year-old buffalo bull," observed Walter R. Morrison, a Texas waddy of the 1800s. As soon as he dropped a loop over the bull's tufted skull, the beast whirled and attacked, forcing the cowpuncher to cut his rope to escape.

"I am here to say that animal was full of fight," Morrison reflected in the late 1930s.

E. A. "Berry" Robuck, going up the trail through Indian Territory in the nineteenth century, also learned that a lassoed bison could challenge even a stout bronc and determined cowhand. Leaping from the saddle after throwing a loop, Robuck went down under flailing hoofs that shredded his shirt, yet he managed to subdue the buffalo with a hobble.

Marvin Hooper, punching cows for the Millard Eidson Ranch near Penwell, Texas, in the early 1930s, discovered that confinement under barbed wire did little to curb a buffalo's aggressive nature. Every time he rode within eyesight of one particular bison cow, the animal charged—once from half a mile away. Still, when Glenn Allen asked him to help doctor a wormy buffalo bull, Hooper never considered shirking his duty.

"That thing was just a-fightin' his shadow," Hooper remembered. "I got my rope down and he made a run at me, and I caught him right around the neck. And this horse I was on was just a-rearin' and a-lungin'."

The bison hit the end of the lariat with choking force that sent the bull sprawling. Allen sprang from the saddle and tied the legs, then signaled Hooper to let his horse give slack in order to free the bison's windpipe. But try as Hooper might, he couldn't force the bronc even a step closer.

"That horse was scared to death, and I was too," Hooper remembered.

By the time Allen cut the rope and pried the loop from the shaggy neck, the buffalo had choked to death.

With bison scarce and owners resistant to unnecessary cattle roping, cowhands tossed loops at just about anything else that moved—wild turkeys, coyotes, antelope, deer. Such prey offered challenge with little peril, but bears or mountain lions could make any roper's hair stand on end.

Sometimes, though, such encounters were more dangerous for animal than cowhand. Charles K. Smith, pushing cattle off a mountain in a long-ago roundup on the Charco de los Marinos Ranch north of Marfa, Texas, flushed a bear from the timber. The encounter excited Smith, for bears were relatively rare on the ranch, but he held to his task and rode on. After the day's branding, however, he returned with several hounds and his uncle, Charlie Jones. The dogs quickly picked up the bear's trail and drove the animal down the slope, with Smith in reckless pursuit astride his cow pony.

"We hit the flat and the bear was in sight, and I outran the dogs and I roped him," Smith recalled. "My uncle Charlie Jones wanted to take him in alive."

Nevertheless, the bear's panic and the horse's efficiency in keeping a taut lariat were too much to overcome.

"While my uncle was tryin' to tie up his mount, the bear choked to death," Smith remembered.

When Andrew Mather's taut lariat likewise choked a lassoed bear into submission in the nineteenth century, the roper jumped from the saddle and killed the immense beast with a knife. On the Chisholm Trail in 1880, Jack Price Borland and a second drover both dropped loops on a half-grown bear, then secured the animal to a sapling by circling in opposite directions. Cutting down the tree, they used it to transport the bear to camp, where drovers made sport of the animal until killing it.

Occasionally, though, a bear threatened to make sport of a cowboy. Sandy Smith, augering in a Colorado bunkhouse one long-ago night, bet a cowhand twenty-five dollars that he could rope a grizzly and control it—an impossibility for a lone roper, as Smith himself later admitted. Nevertheless, he kept up his bluster even as the cowhands set out through mountainous country and burst upon a grizzly. As his companions looked on, Smith gigged his horse after the fleeing bear and closed to within roping distance. When he dropped a loop on the grizzly, the cornered monster whirled on him.

"That critter made for me quicker than a flash of sky fire," Smith recounted. "It had the rope in one paw and its teeth cleared for action. . . . You know what power the bear has in its front legs."

The cowhand realized that spurring his pony away was folly; the grizzly's greater strength would upend the horse at rope's end and leave him at the bear's mercy.

"I guess the boys watching were saying, 'There goes Smith to the eternal range,'" he related. "Well, I just pulled my .44 and put two shots into the bear's head, hitting it between the eyes."

When his fellow waddies rode up, Smith nodded to the dead grizzly. "Boys," he said, "there's the bear all roped and under my control."

On a technicality, Smith had won the wager, but he had come precariously close to losing his life.

Such true-life accounts gave rise to a host of "big bear" stories, which said as much about a cowboy's imagination as they did his real-life exploits. One such yarn by Bill Holcomb told of his pursuit of a bear into a thicket. Dismounting with Winchester in hand, the Texas cowboy searched the brush, to no avail.

"When I come out," claimed Holcomb, "that damned bear was sittin' up on my horse, had my rope down, and was gonna rope me."

Regardless of their veracity, such tales were unforgettable. "You know," reflected Buck Murrah, who once had sat spellbound through Holcomb's account, "that ol' fellow would tell those things like he really believed them."

In a similar story, a cowpuncher told of lassoing a bear, only to see the animal seize the lariat and reel the pony in like a fisherman does a trout. When the cowhand left the stirrups, the bear sprang into the saddle and fled with his horse, never to be seen again.

"Once in a while you'd find some ol' boy [who'd] spout off and tell you lots of these big bear stories, and you knew he was lyin'," observed Bill Townsend, a 1920s cowboy of the Pecos. "But he didn't mean anything by it; he was just entertainin'."

Many wildlife tales, however, had an undeniable ring of truth about them. A case in point was Will Crittendon's encounter with a panther on the Manning Ranch near Terrell, Texas. Twirling his rope as he rode along, he crossed paths with a mountain lion. Giving in to temptation, Crittendon lassoed the cat, only to see the predator spin and advance with gleaming fangs.

"Lawd! Lawd!" he reflected decades later. "I saw what a big mistake I'd made. . . . There was a big post by his path, and he leaped on it so's to make his jump down on me."

Whipping out his six-shooter, Crittendon plugged the panther just in time.

Although attacks on humans by healthy coyotes or wolves in North America are rare—some even say unknown in the case of wolves—such knowledge was of little comfort to an unarmed cowboy stalked by a pack. Anytime predators lost their natural fear of man, it called for alarm. Even so, a cowhand had to keep his trepidation in check, lest fear itself become the greater enemy.

One night as Lonnie Griffith rode across a West Texas pasture bathed in moonlit haze, his trailing packhorse suddenly jumped and rushed abreast. Spinning, Griffith saw the phantom of a coyote within ten feet of the pony's hindquarter.

"I knew good and well that coyote had nipped that horse on the leg," Griffith remembered. "My horse jumped too—both horses was wantin' to run."

A coyote in a trap on the Three Circle Ranch in Texas in 1906. (E. E. Smith Collection, Nita Stewart Haley Memorial Library, Midland, Texas)

Checking the night, Griffith found three coyotes on one side and two more shadows on the other. "Them coyotes wasn't afraid of me—they had me flanked in, just kinda trottin'," he recounted. "By gosh, that got me scared, I'll tell you that. 'Cause if that horse had throwed me, I didn't know what was gonna happen."

For three miles, the coyotes skulked alongside as Griffith fought to control his terrified bronc. The two ponies were roped together, and to let them break into a run could spawn a wreck that would leave him vulnerable to attack.

"I just didn't know what time them coyotes was gonna close in and start tryin' to get them horses," remembered the cowhand.

After an eternity, Griffith reached a gate, and the predators disappeared into the night. "That bunch of coyotes, I believe, intended to do somethin' to me, but they just never did get nerve enough," he reflected.

In an earlier era, wolves could chill the marrow of a cowboy set afoot, especially if he laid a trail of blood with every step. In 1867 cattle drover "One-Armed Bill" Wilson, his bare feet bleeding, staggered half-dead down the Pecos after an Indian attack in southeastern New Mexico. A slug had felled his companion, Oliver Loving, and Wilson had set off on a desperate search for help. Yet now, armed with only a walking stick, the one-armed cowhand faced a night as terrifying as the rain of arrows and lead three days before.

"The wolves followed me all night," Wilson recalled many years later. "I would give out, just like a horse, and lay down in the road and drop off to sleep, and when I would awaken the wolves would be all around me, snapping and snarling."

Each time, Wilson would seize the stick and fight off the fangs, but the wolves evidently sensed that he was ready for the kill. As soon as he would drag himself up and stumble on through the shadows, they would follow relentlessly, a pack of demons determined to bring him down. Wilson managed to endure the horrid cycle until daybreak, when the wolves finally slunk away into the Pecos desert.

Of all creatures a cowboy might face, a rattlesnake was the most dreaded. Although its venomous fangs could write his epitaph with a flashing strike, a waddy usually harbored a loathing entirely out of proportion to the chances of that happening. As was the case with many men through the ages, rattlesnakes could engender in cowhands an irrational fear as old as Eden.

"There were two things that the cowboys were deathly afraid of," noted Texas cowpoke L. M. Cox, "and that was the Pecos River and rattlesnakes."

Bill Townsend's dark night alone in a Texas bunkhouse speaks volumes about a typical cowpuncher's fear of rattlers. Asleep, the top hand stirred to a howling wind and the staccato of maracas just outside his door.

"It was a big one—you could tell by the way he was rattling," he recalled. "He'd quit, and then I'd hear him again."

Even protected by a closed door, Townsend couldn't overcome his anxiety. "I lay there and the sweat just popped out on me," he admitted.

A cowhand's concern was often multiplied a thousand fold when he slept on the ground, a necessity during a roundup or trail drive. As a preventive measure, he might encircle his bedroll with a rope, for folklore had it that a rattler wouldn't crawl across a lariat. But unlike a canvas barrier, which at least could discourage rabid skunks, a rope had no more chance of warding off reptiles than a cowboy did of lassoing the wind.

If a sleeping cowhand did find an unwelcome visitor, only incredible self-control could suppress his natural instinct to panic. The prudent response was to lie still until the snake slithered away, no matter how long it might take. Any attempt at fight or flight could provoke a strike, yet cuddling with a rattlesnake demanded a level of courage, patience, and stamina that few cowboys possessed. Around cow camps, "big rattler" stories became almost as popular a way to boast of one's virility as "big bear" stories.

"I woke up one mornin' and a big ol' rattlesnake was coiled up on my chest," Texas cowman Ad Horek once drawled. "He was lookin' me right in the eye. He stuck out his tongue and licked me on the chin. I just went back to sleep. Next time I woke up, he was gone."

Maybe it happened that way, and maybe it didn't, but some cowhands did exhibit amazing control in this most trying of circumstances. Anytime the situation evoked restraint in multiple cowpunchers, the incident was truly memorable.

A common practice in cow camps was to "cut bedding," or share a bedroll, but in South Texas one night about 1926, Otis Coggins and a second cowhand found themselves cutting bedding three ways instead of two. Far into the night, the second waddy roused Coggins with a frantic whisper.

"Lay still, Otis! Lay still!"

Even a groggy Coggins could detect alarm in his friend's voice. "What's the matter?" Coggins asked.

"There's a rattlesnake crawlin' across us!"

Sure enough, through two blankets and a wagon sheet, Coggins could feel the rattler's every squirm. Nevertheless, he had no choice but to lie motionless until the reptile slithered away, at which point the men scrambled up and killed the intruder by lantern light.

Bedrolls awaiting unwelcome visitors on El Capitan Land and Cattle Company's Three Block Ranch in New Mexico in 1908 or 1909. Pictured are Jim Finch, J. F. Weissienger, and L. Taylor. (E. E. Smith Collection, Nita Stewart Haley Memorial Library, Midland, Texas)

More commonly, a cowboy didn't tarry for an instant upon learning of an uninvited guest in his bedroll. Indeed, with the frenzy of a quail flushed from a bush, he usually flung the covers and dashed for Jericho. If he was lucky, he might find the rattler before ever joining it in repose, although such a find might haunt him every time he reclined thereafter. How would he ever know that he hadn't snuggled with the rattler the night before? And if he didn't know, how could he be certain that there wasn't another one in his bed this very moment?

Such thoughts probably troubled a Spade cowhand after he once unfurled his bedroll in the West Texas dirt and found an eighteen-inch rattlesnake inside. In the chill of the previous night, the cold-blooded reptile apparently had sought warmth in the blankets. Rolled in the bedding when the cowhands had broken camp, the snake had gone undetected even as the cook had tossed the bedroll in the wagon for a jarring ride to this new location.

Texas cowpoke Carl Earp, unrolling his bed at a McElroy Ranch wagon camp one night in the 1930s, was startled by a harmless prairie snake. Earp's reaction, however, was just as animated as if it had been a venomous diamondback; he whooped and jumped and danced away. But the snake also exhibited plenty of vigor.

"It sure kicked up some dust getting away from there," recalled Paul Patterson, who witnessed the incident. "He was just as glad to get away as Carl was to see him get away."

Even on a line-shack porch, a cowhand's bedding wasn't immune to vipers. Outside an X outfit bunkhouse in Trans-Pecos Texas one summer in the early 1920s, a tired cowboy lay down for well-deserved rest, only to recoil at a chilling vibration between blankets and planks. Out slithered a rattlesnake, spurring the man into flight.

The thrill of discovery was never pleasant when it came to rattle-tails. All through a frigid night at a 7D wagon camp in West Texas in the mid-1930s, Nig Brown slept contentedly in his bedroll, but when morning broke and he stretched under the covers, he stuck his feet in something cold.

"Boy, he come out of there in a hurry," recalled Charlie Drennan, whose own bedding lay nearby.

When Brown shook out his blankets, he found a rattlesnake with eight rattles.

Such a find usually prompted every other cowhand in camp to check his own bedroll, for rattlers often came in pairs, a lesson Slim Armentrout learned the hard way in the 1930s. Sound asleep on a trail drive through West Texas, the waddy stirred to a frantic cry in the night—"Rattlesnake!"

"I jumped up, and there was a rattlesnake down there with me in my bed," Armentrout remembered. "There was another one in somebody else's bed. They was just rolling around there, rattling. Didn't bite nobody, but I got out of there."

W. H. Thomas, a Texas cowpoke born in 1870, recalled several unwelcome bed partners in his years sleeping under the stars. "I've woke up with sand rattlers and diamondbacks too," he noted. "Long as you didn't hurt them, they wouldn't bite you. . . . I never rolled in my sleep because I was so tired when I went to bed that I just wanted to lay still and rest."

Impersonating a statue may have been all that saved a South Texas cowhand named Frank on a daylight cattle drive in the 1920s or 1930s. When the drovers stopped for a few minutes of shut-eye, Frank sat back against a tree and soon was snoring. Leonard Hernandez, dozing nearby, awakened to Frank's quiet whistle. Looking over, Hernandez was perplexed by the cowhand's actions.

"He kept on whistlin' and a-pointin', but he wouldn't move anything but his hand," Hernandez recounted. "Them other boys would say, 'Well, do it yourself, so-and-so.' But Frank kept whisperin' 'Hey!'"

Frank had good reason for his antics—a rattler was coiled right between his legs. When he finally made his predicament known, a cowhand approached and popped a bullwhip, which induced the snake to uncoil and crawl away.

Whether asleep or awake, afoot or astride, a cowboy in rattlesnake country was always at risk. Jimmy Yiser, caught in the saddle amid a swarm of sunning rattlers in West Texas in the 1950s, could only give the horse its head and let it tiptoe to safety. Sometimes, though, a pony wasn't so lucky; Texas puncher Ben Kinchlow was in the stirrups one day when a striking rattler hung its fangs in his bronc's leg.

"My hoss reared an' plunged till he stepped on the snake with his hind foot an' pulled the snake loose," he remembered.

When another horse once sustained a bite on the Texas range, Paul Patterson and a Mexican cowhand administered first aid. The treatment was so painful that the four-year-old stallion reared and pawed, striking Patterson in the head with its knee and knocking him out.

"When I came to, I couldn't see anything—I thought I'd been knocked blind too," Patterson related.

Fortunately, Patterson suffered only obscured vision; his superstitious companion had covered his face with a shirt in the belief that too much fresh air upon awakening would kill him.

As with many cowboys, Patterson encountered rattlesnakes in every way imaginable. One September night about 1930, he went outside to undertake a ranch chore and stepped on a four-and-a-half-foot rattler. "I knew by the way my foot rolled that I was on a snake," he recalled. Fortunately, the viper didn't strike.

Luck was also on the Texas cowpoke's side one day in the late 1920s when he dismounted to quench his thirst at a rain-filled grinding hole on King Mountain. Sprawling prone to sip, Patterson had yet to bear weight on his stomach when another cowhand cried out.

Six-foot, two-inch Bob McClellan displaying a rattler killed at the Spade Headquarters Ranch in Texas in the 1920s or 1930s. (Photo courtesy of Fred McClellan)

"A . . . a . . . a . . . snake! You-you're on a snake!"

The warning came just in time. "I looked down and saw a little ol' rattlesnake about eighteen inches long right under me, just plum' under me," Patterson recounted. "If I'd've let down on my belly, he'd've bit me. He just crawled on out of the way."

Even killing a rattlesnake proved perilous to Patterson about 1930 in the Ozona country of Texas. Spying a healthy specimen, he dismounted and whipped it with the double of a rope. As he jerked the lariat back, the reptile was attached and came flying at him, forcing Patterson to dive aside to avoid a rattler about his neck.

Fred McClellan could thank his chaps for sparing him when he once dismounted on the Spade Ranch to kill a Texas diamondback. Focusing on the reptile as he approached with a doubled rope, he never saw the second rattler until it struck him on his leggings. In a late-1910s incident, young Billy Rankin of Texas also reaped the reward of stout leather chaps as he stood ready to stone a rattler. When another cowhand seized the snake by the tail and popped it like a whip, the head flew off and the fangs buried in Rankin's leggings.

"If it hadn't've killed the snake, I'd've drug it to death runnin'," Rankin reflected.

Coping with a live rattler dangling from one's person was probably a cowhand's least favorite pastime. When W. F. Kellis's bronc bolted through West Texas mesquites about 1887 and the thorns shredded his trousers, he never guessed that it had set the stage for an unforgettable episode. Riding to a general store in the small settlement of Montvale, Kellis purchased the only pair of pants in stock—a size forty, even though he wore only a thirty-one.

"The seat of these breeches, after I was in them, had room for a [whole] family," he recalled. "Truly, they hung low and wide as I rode off to a roundup on Lacy Creek."

En route, Kellis had to cross a steep mountain. Starting down the far side, he found the slope so treacherous that he dismounted and led his horse. As he stepped off a line of rimrock, his bronc shied and yanked back on the reins. For a moment, the cowhand was suspended, with one foot on the ledge and the other stretched over open space. From directly below, a hidden rattler struck and hung its fangs in the roomy seat of his britches.

"Dropping my bridle reins, I went down that mountain at a rate that any modern speed fool might envy," Kellis recounted. "I was yelling, 'Snake! Snake!' just as if I expected to be heard, and I don't suppose there was a human being within five miles of me. I turned somersaults and rolled and kicked . . . , but that booger held right on."

Finally Kellis leaped a thorny catclaw bush and dislodged the rattler, but he continued his madcap dash down the mountain.

"I have often shuddered to think what might have happened had I not had on my big, baggy breeches," Kellis reflected in 1937. "I have dreamed of that snake at least a hundred times, always awakening with a severe case of the jitters."

In 1900, a cowhand earned the sobriquet "Snaky Joe" after a similar encounter during a roundup in Howard County, Texas. Awakening to find that his mount had escaped its hobble, Joe took up his lariat and went in search. When he plunged a boot into a prairie dog hole, a waiting rattler struck him in the ankle. Doctoring the bite with a stream of tobacco juice, he continued on a short distance before sitting down to reassess his condition. By doing so, he only made his predicament worse, for he plopped in the middle of a second rattler.

Unaware of its presence, Joe finally stood, confident that he suffered no ill effects from the bite. But now, the second rattler dangled from his trousers seat and continued to cling even as the cowhand caught his bronc.

Joe managed to saddle the animal, but the horse refused to cooperate as he tried to mount. The cowboy couldn't understand—until the tug of the squirming rattler induced him to check the rear of his britches.

"Yow!"

Still clutching the reins, Joe fled like a dog trying to outrun its tail. His antics caught the attention of Red Wiggins, who initially found the sight so comical that he couldn't control his laughter. But when the bronc began to trample the cowboy, Wiggins sprang to his rescue, seizing the horse and freeing the snake from its hold. As soon as Wiggins related the incident around the chuck wagon, the nickname "Snaky Joe" was set in stone.

Memorable, scary, revolting—brushes with rattlers or other wild spawn could be any of these to a cowhand going about his job. In terms of threat, however, nature's denizens always paled before the awesome manifestations of nature's wrath.

Screaming Rocks and Sky Fire

Friends were true and stood with each other till the very last in any difficulty.

—John M. Hardeman, cowhand

The very nature of a cowboy's profession demanded that he challenge the elements. Like the proverbial postman, neither rain, nor snow, nor heat, nor gloom of night could keep him from his appointed rounds. If the sky didn't cooperate, so be it, but he had a job to do and do it he would, despite hell or high water. In the ballgame that was his life, there were neither rain-outs nor rain delays, only relentless seasons under skies dictated by nature's whim. By summer, he faced heatstroke with no more protection than a broad-brimmed Stetson, while by winter, he braved threats of sometimes unimaginable proportions.

"It was a terror," Mose Hayes said of a South Plains blizzard in 1886. "A man couldn't face it."

The winters of 1883 and 1884 in the Red River country were equally fierce. "We would simply freeze right through to the marrow, it seemed," noted Spence Hardie. "It was so cold that grown men cried and never thought anything about it."

Caught out overnight, Hardie not only built roaring fires on either side, but repeatedly moved the fires in order to keep his bedroll on the residual hot ashes. "We didn't dare to go to sleep, for it might be the last sleep we'd ever have," he observed.

In a deep snow, a horse might plunge with its rider into a hidden cavity, placing both in the kind of jeopardy M. A. Withers knew so well. Riding through a Nevada snow, the drover plummeted in the saddle into a white-shrouded prospector's dig, necessitating a rescue by rope. Even sleet could take a toll on a rider, sometimes numbing him beyond his ability to dismount on his own.

Whether in Nevada or Texas, New Mexico or Montana, the combination of bitter cold and driving winds could freeze exposed flesh in seconds. In 1894, a pitiless blizzard caught drovers unawares as they crossed the TX range near the Pecos River in Texas. As night fell, the desperate men tried to set fire to a rat's den, but none of them could grasp a match in the gnawing cold. Before they climbed back in the saddle by day, they insulated their boots with gunny sacks—a precaution that spared them the fate of a TX cowhand who froze both feet.

In a later incident, a howling blizzard seized M. C. Manuel and another rider on the Bar X range in southeastern New Mexico. The two men made camp and huddled against the cold, but by the time the snowstorm relented three days later, Manuel's feet were so frozen that he narrowly avoided amputation.

Sometimes a cowhand fared even worse. When ferocious winds struck a remote line shack on the Spade Ranch in the Texas Panhandle in January 1918, M. F. "Mart" Driver opened the door to a blizzard from hell. With conditions deteriorating quickly, the lone cowhand knew he had to take immediate action to save twenty-six calves, ranging from three days to two weeks old.

"The poor little things just looked as if they would freeze when the wind first hit them," he recalled.

Braving winds of forty to fifty miles per hour, Driver took a wagon through the piling snow in search of the herd—a testament to a cowboy's sense of duty. Lassoing the calves, he loaded them in the wagon and headed back to camp, where the animals would have better protection.

"About the time I got the calves all up, I began to suffer with my head and face," Driver remembered. "My jaws went to aching until I could hardly stand it when I went out in the wind."

Still, he had to check the welfare of the cows, a responsibility that drove him repeatedly into the pasture as the blizzard continued its siege. Four or five days later, his face and jaws were so frostbitten that he sent for help by way of a passerby.

"My face was swollen and paining me so badly that I wanted to have my teeth extracted," he remembered. After Driver finally reached town, he got his wish—a dentist nursed the cowboy's gums back to a semblance of health, then pulled all his teeth.

Sometimes a winter storm was so treacherous that a cowboy such as Driver had to rein in his almost incredible passion for his job. On the trail for Dodge City, Kansas, in 1876, drovers rode into a blizzard punctuated by freezing rain. The cold was more than they could bear, but every hand stayed with the herd until the trail boss shouted the only thing that prudence allowed.

"Let 'em go to hell, boys, and we'll go to the campfire!"

Even after skies turned bright, the glare of sunlight on a white wonderland could literally blind a cowboy. Perry A. Burgess, herding cattle in the Montana snows in 1867, first experienced disturbing symptoms on March 3.

"My eyes are very weak and painful," he wrote in his diary. "Cannot see well."

By the next day, Burgess's vision had diminished to the point that another cowhand helped him on his horse and guided him to a line shack. Burgess was perplexed by his ailment until a man and his wife told him he was snow-blind.

"Could not see to fix my victuals at the table," Burgess scribbled that day. "They put the grub on my plate and cut it into mouthfuls as they would for a yearling child."

Blind as "a stone" and sequestered in a dark room, Burgess endured two days of severe pain before improving, but it wasn't until March 9 that he was able to don goggles and climb back in the saddle.

Teddy Blue Abbott, blinded in the snows of Montana, faced a similar ordeal: Confined to bed with salt poultices over his eyes, he suffered five days of pain so intense that he could neither sleep nor eat.

Rivaling snow-blindness for agony was a pounding levied by hard, white rocks from the sky. Hail was dreaded especially on the plains, where a rider's only protection was his garb. His slicker sufficed against pea-sized hail, while marble-sized stones did little more than beat out an annoying cadence on his hat. But hailstones of greater diameter—especially if driven by fierce winds—could make a cowboy cringe, and if they approached the size of a fist, they could shatter his skull.

"The beat of the hail on my head made me crazy," said one drover of an 1871 storm in Bosque County, Texas. "I would have run but didn't know which way to go."

With escape impossible, the best a cowhand could hope for in the worst of hailstorms was merely to survive, and even then he was sure to sustain welts and bruises that would torture him for days. "Fo' a week after, we-uns squeal like pigs when we-uns tries to move fast, 'cause of de sore spots," cowhand James Cape said of a brutal pummeling on the trail from Mexico to Texas.

A cowboy's hands, if exposed, were particularly susceptible to bruising, but a numbing blow to the hand could have another consequence—it could shatter his grip on the reins. Abbott, night-guarding a herd on the North Platte in 1883, endured a frightful battering astride his horse until a hailstone caught his fist.

"It hurt so bad I let go the reins as he plunged," he wrote. "The rest of the night I was afoot and helpless."

A fastball-of-a-hailstone could also bloody a cowboy's face, fracture a limb, or wreak havoc with a joint. After a hailstorm in the North Concho River country of Texas in 1890, one cowboy even sought treatment from a Montvale doctor for a dislocated shoulder.

The degree of a hailstorm's fury could be measured by its toll on livestock and wildlife, and any storm that reached the rabbit-killing stage was certain to punish a cowhand. In one such maelstrom west of Midland, Texas, in 1888, a bald cowboy apparently lost his hat as countless jackrabbits dropped around him. "He was a sight to behold," recalled Jerry M. Nance, a fellow drover. "He had welts and bruises all over, and lots of hide had been peeled off."

If a hailstorm rose to the level of an antelope or yearling killer, a cowboy had reason to fear for his life. On the afternoon of July 4, 1880, a black storm swooped down on the Arkansas River and engulfed a trail outfit. "[It was] the awfulest hailstorm . . . a man ever saw," reflected G. W. Mills, a drover. "The hailstones nearly beat us to death; it knocked over jackrabbits like taking them off with a rifle. It even killed a few yearlings and many fleet antelopes."

Through a choking daytime darkness, the cowhands stayed at their posts, taking it on the chin and shivering from a piercing cold. Night fell, and still the riders clung to the herd, the ice crunching underfoot as they drifted ten miles with the boogered cattle. When day broke and the cowboys rode for the chuck wagon, four inches of hail still shrouded the ground—an ice storm in summer. Finally, at ten o'clock, the scourged men pulled rein before the astonished cook, who already had consigned them to a tragic end.

"We found the cook fixing to leave, thinking surely that all the men had been killed," remembered Mills.

If a hailstorm raged so fiercely that it felled even mature cattle, a rider had no choice but to abandon his stirrups before a screaming white rock knocked him senseless. He had one chance—yank the saddle off and huddle under the stout leather. J. R. Walkup and his fellow drovers, forced to such a measure in nineteenth-century Wyoming, weathered an onslaught that claimed twenty cattle and two horses. After a similar brush with hell on the Texas plains, J. P. Benard shed his saddle and counted seventy-five cattle carcasses.

Above Fort Sumner, New Mexico, in 1893, drovers with an M. Halff & Brother herd encountered a hailstorm so violent that it defied categorization. Indeed, it may have been the deadliest in the history of cattle drives. When the beleaguered men cast aside their sheltering saddles, they stared in amazement at a white plain strewn with carcasses—almost six hundred two-year-old steers, as well as virtually every horse in the remuda. Set afoot in an unforgiving land, the drovers had to send for help in Texas before they could continue north with the surviving cattle.

Winds, which often roared in concert with hailstorms, could be treacherous in their own right, especially if they took the form of straight-line events or tornadoes. "The wind was so strong at times it nearly blew me out of the saddle," E. A. "Berry" Robuck said of one storm in Indian Territory. In Kansas in 1869, another shrieking blast rocked a grove of trees in which several waddies were camped. L. D. Taylor anchored himself to a stump and clung for dear life, while the trail boss secured his own death grip on a nearby sapling.

"His feet were constantly in my way, flying around and striking my shins and knocking the bark off the stump I was hanging to," recalled Taylor. "The wind would pick us up and flop our bodies against the ground with great force."

With strength born of desperation, the men held on and survived, but sometimes even the stoutest tree wouldn't have been enough to neutralize a windstorm. As a spinning black rope dropped from an ominous cloud in Dakota Territory in 1871, drovers in position around a herd didn't know what to make of it; none of them had ever seen a tornado. But when the cyclone struck the ground and began to mill and twist a path of destruction, they knew exactly what to do—put spurs to horses!

"Right there, we let the cattle take care of themselves, and every man made a run to get out of the path of the twister," remembered E. P. Byler. Only by the narrowest of margins did the drovers escape.

An underestimated threat to a cowhand racked by storm was flash flooding. Although so inured to hardship that he could sleep soundly as rain pounded his tarp and water stood around him, a cowpuncher never relished forking a horse under such conditions. With water pooling across the landscape, a rider could no longer distinguish solid footing from flooded dog hole or surging ravine, and even his horse's normally reliable instincts were of no help. Will King, taking his mount through sheetlike rain on the Smoky River in Kansas one night in 1874, almost drowned when his animal stepped off into a rushing arroyo.

Of all weather-related perils, "sky fire" was the most awe inspiring and lethal, a threat so mysterious and sovereign that it could strike terror in even the most courageous of cowhands. Like the finger of God descending in judgment, lightning could surge in an instant from boiling, black clouds that reverberated with a crescendo like the cries of the damned. On the plains, a bolt would target a man on horseback before anything else—reason enough, if a cowhand needed any more reason, to dread this uncanny force with an unspeakable fear.

Nineteen-year-old John B. Conner, night-herding the remuda during an 1885 thunderstorm on the Salt Fork of Red River, panicked as he studied the horses' reactions. They bunched around him, sheltered their heads between their knees, and began to moan. "I became frightened and decided that the end of time had come," he

Lightning streaking the Texas sky. (Photo courtesy of Richard Galle)

related. "I thought I was as brave as any man, but the action of the horses was too much for me."

Expecting a fatal strike any moment, the desperate wrangler escaped the stirrups and threw himself flat on the ground. "I tried to die but could not," he remembered. "The storm passed on."

In a job that demanded self-sufficiency and precluded church-going, cowboys were seldom religious, but sky fire was better than a camp meeting for getting men to pray. As an electrical storm enveloped four night riders on an 1880 drive to Indian Territory, one cowhand kept railing that they would all be killed. His fear was contagious, prompting Bill Hancock to whirl to Jim Wilson.

"Did you ever pray?" asked Hancock.

"No," admitted Wilson, "not in a long time."

"Some of us have got to pray!" Hancock pressed. "The lightning's going to kill all of us!"

The storm intensified, lightning strikes exploding on all sides. In the tumult, the four riders became separated, forcing each man to face alone a dark world of chaos and uncertainty.

"When our crowd got together again," Wilson recalled four decades later, "we found Bill off his horse praying aloud."

Prayer seemed the only thing that might spare a man from lightning at its most destructive—when rapid-fire bolts kept an entire herd illuminated at midnight, when the tall-grass prairie erupted like the flames of perdition, when concentrated hell bombed hillsides and gouged great holes. But whether stupendous or subtle, horrific or possessing evil beauty, electrical displays always burned themselves into a cowboy's memory. R. C. Burns, riding guard over a herd one night, witnessed the full range of sky fire's wonders in a single thunderstorm.

"It commenced like flash lightning, then becomes forked lightning, then chain lightning, followed by the peculiar blue lightning," he recounted. "It rapidly developed into ball lightning, which rolled along the ground, and after that, spark lightning."

The most chilling moment came when eerie electricity settled over the scene like a fog.

"The air smelled of burning sulfur," he remembered. "You could see it on the horns of the cattle, the ears of our horses, and the brims of our hats. It grew so warm that we thought we would be burned up."

When a thunderstorm threatened, a cowhand had few options. He might toss aside his six-shooter, and maybe his spurs and pocketknife, in the hope that the absence of metal would make him less of a target. If on horseback, he could lower his profile by dismounting. Even so, if he chose to hold to the reins rather than creep away, the horse could draw a strike fatal to both. But setting himself afoot on purpose—especially in a storm that could scatter his herd—went against the grain of every responsible cowhand.

One thing a prudent cowboy didn't want to do was take refuge under a tree—especially one that stood alone—but sometimes it took tragedy to teach such a lesson. When a hard rain deluged a northbound herd near the San Marcos River in Texas one night in 1870, drover Ran Spencer and a waddy named Fly rode for sheltering branches, despite a sky rent by jagged lightning. When the storm relented and they failed to report to the wagon, fellow cowhands searched the dark.

"We found Spencer sitting [dead] against a tree, his head drooped down just like he was asleep," said W. R. Massengale. "Fly had his head on Spencer's legs and was struck also, but did not die until next day."

Even a cow camp was not immune to a strike; indeed, a wagon rising from a prairie was a prime candidate, especially considering the irons and cookery. In separate incidents in 1878, lightning stunned a cook near Sydney, Nebraska, and another bolt dropped five cowhands and killed seven horses in a camp forty miles south of Cheyenne, Wyoming. A similar strike near Dallas in 1868 killed one cowboy in camp and seared three others.

A thunderstorm posed so great a dilemma for a rider that he often just stayed in the saddle, sort of an Old West Russian roulette. If sky fire fell and he was as lucky as A. Huffmeyer in 1878, only his horse would be affected. Riding herd in a dreadful thunderstorm at Red River Station, Huffmeyer cringed to an explosion that killed nine cattle alongside him.

"It stunned my horse and he fell to the ground but was up in an instant and ready to go," he remembered.

The crash of a nearby strike could echo for days in a rider's ears. "I liked to got killed by lightning the other night," drover W. D.

Connell wrote from Hereford, Texas, on May 27, 1903. "It killed two of my steers right by me. Didn't hurt me any, just made my ears ring a little."

Frequently in such a situation, streamer currents would jolt a rider, sometimes severely enough to fell him. "I was knocked off my horse by it twice," noted Teddy Blue Abbott. "The first time, I saw a ball of fire coming toward me and felt something strike me on the head." When he came to, he was lying under his horse and rain was pelting his face.

All too often, the strike of lightning committed a rider to a lonely grave along some forgotten trail far from home. The victim of a direct hit was often so gruesome a sight that the image could haunt his fellow cowhands, who realized that the dead man's fate might be their own someday. As Gus Johnson, G. B. Withers, and M. A. Withers rode for camp near Dodge City, Kansas, in 1882, a thunderbolt exploded among them and knocked the latter man from his horse. Shaken but uninjured, he checked his companions and found G. B. Withers blinded in one eye and Johnson sprawled dead.

"It set Johnson's undershirt on fire, and his gold shirt stud, which was set with a diamond, was melted," M. A. Withers recalled. "His hat was torn to pieces, and mine had all the plush burned off of the top."

More than clothing evidenced Billie Ballard's violent end astride a cow pony after lightning struck him near Knickerbocker, Texas, in the spring of 1890. "Ballard's head," reported the May 24, 1890, *Texas Live Stock Journal*, "was bursted open and his clothing entirely torn from his body."

No cowhand relished such a fate, but even if he avoided incredible voltage, he still might end up just as dead if a terrified herd bolted at lightning's sudden crack.

Clashing Horns

There is something about riding the range and dealing with the danger of a stampede. . . . All that gets into a fellow's blood.

—Robert W. Keen, cowhand

A Matador Ranch herd on the march in Texas in 1910. (E. E. Smith Collection, Nita Stewart Haley Memorial Library, Midland, Texas)

A stampede was a stupendous engine of destruction unlike anything else a cowboy ever faced. A dynamic force not to be denied, it multiplied the threat of a single cow brute by thousands and often materialized under extreme conditions that forced a cowhand to acts of brash courage. Through a night rent by sky fire or across pitch-black plains riddled with gullies and prairie dog holes, he put spurs to horse and rode hell-bent for election to save herd and pride.

"What if there was thunder and lightning and hail and they run damn near all night?" reflected Teddy Blue Abbott in 1931. "We would swing with the lead and throw them into a mill and sing to them. Wasn't we hired to carry that herd up North? And we sure as hell done it."

With most stampedes occurring after a trail herd bedded down, drovers kept vigil throughout the night. Off-duty cowhands, exhausted after long hours in the saddle, wanted nothing more than to seek a dead man's sleep in camp, fifty to a few hundred yards away. Yet a waddy never unrolled his blankets without first staking a saddled horse nearby. On a moment's notice, he could join the night riders, who did their best to avert trouble by slowly circling the herd and calming the animals with quiet song. In one shift or another between dusk and dawn, each drover in the outfit stood guard, sometimes with eyelids so heavy that he rubbed them with tobacco, an irritant certain to keep him awake.

Suddenly, to a clap of thunder or to the strike of a match or from an impetus not understood, trouble erupted. Maybe only a single critter spooked, but its fear seemed to spread instantly through the entire herd. To a drowsy rider, the precipitous upspring of thousands of shadowy cattle looked as if the very earth were heaving, but the ensuing maelstrom was more likely to evoke comparisons with perdition.

"They acted just as if the devil had jumped right up in the middle of them and hollered, 'Boo!'" said cowhand W. H. Thomas. Corroborated another Texas drover, W. B. Currie: "It seemed like hell was bustin' wide open."

Bust wide open it did, with such speed and fury that only reminiscing cowhands could capture the moment in all its ominous majesty.

"With a rush like a whirlwind that levels a forest, they were off in the darkness, the strong ones in the lead," said Utah cowman Bob Heywood in 1883.

"They was just crazy with fear," noted Gus Schroeder, a Northwest cowboy. "You never heard such a racket in your life, what with their runnin' on that hard open ground, their bellowin' and their horns crashin'! Their horns crashin' was the worst. You wouldn't think they could make so much noise."

"[It] would sound as though hell had turned all its imps loose," summarized Gaston Fergenson, a Texas waddy born in 1861.

As the stampede swept across the land like a tidal wave, thousands of flinty hoofs pulverized underlying vegetation and churned the turf, leaving a straight, smooth swath "cut as if by a mowing machine," described Heywood. The night guards couldn't escape the fray even if they wanted, for their horses would go wild, jumping and running at the same moment as the herd. If ever there was a time for caution, it was now, but there was also never a situation that demanded such reckless daring.

Imagine chasing down the leaders through a storm-wrenched night, then crowding a skittish horse against rapier-like horns of terrified demons, all in a desperate attempt to turn the elongated herd back in on itself and force a mill, the only chance of stopping a stampede. Add to this grim scenario the fact that a cowhand had to ride "at a dead run in the dark, with cut banks and prairie dog holes all around you, not knowing if the next jump would land you in a shallow grave," as Abbott declared—and only then might a city slicker have some inkling of the challenges and perils of a stampede rider. Such a moment required more than a mere cowpuncher; it demanded a top hand with plenty of "sand in his gizzard," as drovers were wont to say.

"A cowhand was playing with Lady Luck every minute of the run," reflected drover James Childers, who rode with abandon in Indian Territory.

When the range shook to hoofbeats, the rushing horde's gliding shadow dictated a horseman's course as he came up alongside. In brushy country, a flanking rider was exposed to outlying limbs that could explode out of the dark. If he managed to stay in the saddle, he could expect a scourging that he wouldn't soon forget. After one such stampede near Cotulla, Texas, in the mid-1880s, the drovers looked as if they "had been to an Irish wake, all bloody and bruised," remembered George W. Brock. Texas cowhand J. G.

Riders flanking a Matador Ranch herd on a 1910 drive in Texas. (E. E. Smith Collection, Nita Stewart Haley Memorial Library, Midland, Texas)

Mooring, who once endured a similar flogging, was even more graphic: "All of us had left yards of hide hanging on the brush."

The punishment was severe enough to drive some victimized cowhands to regions far removed. Abbott, his face and hands bloodied in an 1883 stampede south of San Antonio, vowed never to return to the South Texas Brush Country. "I was a bloody sight," wrote Abbott, who made good on his promise. "My knees was the worst of all. I was picking thorns out of them all the way to Kansas."

To a rider's alarm, he might find himself pinned between the herd's flank and a precipice, a predicament that could turn deadly if the beeves crowded him. W. A. Tinney, facing such a dilemma in the Blanco country of Texas one night, had plenty of motivation as he fought to veer the leaders.

"I often think of what a spot I was in," Tinney noted years later. "It's dangerous enough to be out in front of a stampeding herd of crazy cow critters, but to have that arroyo facing you too, that's a stumper for sure."

Sometimes even an experienced cowhand never realized what he could achieve until he had no other choice. Tinney succeeded in turning the leaders and avoided a dangerous wreck, but other riders met with disaster under such circumstances. On an 1880s night so black that stampede chasers rode blind across a Texas range, George W. Brock and Russ Jones came abreast of the leaders on opposite sides and fought each other's efforts to turn the beeves. Unfortunately for Brock, whose horse was skirting a ditch six feet deep, Jones won out. When the leaders swung toward Brock, his horse had no place to go but in the gully. The impact was crushing, but the cowhand somehow eluded injury.

In a similar accident on the trail to Kansas in 1870, a thousand raging cattle forced Jesse Jolly off a bluff overlooking a creek. "My horse turned a complete somersault down into the water, throwing me against a cottonwood tree," he related.

Even if a rider avoided some pitfall on his outside flank, his hurtling pony was always just a stride away from a wreck that could maim or kill or throw him into the path of an unstoppable flood.

"Anyone who never had the experience of a horse falling in the dark of the blackest night with the rain falling in torrents with a deafening crash of thunder every few minutes, the roar of 2,000 cattle scared to distraction, cannot visualize the thoughts of one in that predicament," noted Texas waddy B. A. Oden. "I could [almost] feel my body beat to a pulp by thousands of hoofs."

All a cowhand could do was trust his horse and put himself "in the hands of Jupiter," as drover J. G. Mooring observed. If a rider survived, probably no one would ever thank him, and if he met his end, it would be with the unheralded dignity of a cowboy—with boots on and giving his job its due, rather than wasting away to infirmity or old age.

If a bronc spilled and a cowhand was lucky, he might ride it to the ground and up again, losing only moments in the chase. In an 1871 stampede on the San Marcos River in Texas, jostling cattle dropped J. M. Hankins's pony three times, but the cowhand managed to stay astride throughout. More often when a horse stumbled, its rider flew from the saddle to suffer at least bruised pride.

"My first thought was that the joy and pleasure of the continuance of the trip was gone," said J. R. Humphrie, who evaded injury in an 1880s horse wreck during a stampede on the Kansas trail.

When B. Vesper shook away the cobwebs after a similar fall in Texas in 1870, the herd already had disappeared in the night. He remounted and started for camp, only to lose his bearings. After a long, fruitless ride through a wilderness haunted by howling coyotes, the exhausted waddy took refuge in a tree. Dozing, he lost his grip and fell, awakening in time to seize a lower branch and spare himself two tumbles in the same night.

Sometimes, a stampede victim never remembered his horse going down, despite lasting effects. After Kansas-bound cattle ceased a thundering run in Llano County, Texas, in 1886, drovers found a dazed R. J. Jennings astride his horse in the middle of the herd. "I had in some manner been painfully injured, and for two weeks afterward I could sleep only when I was leaning against the end gate of the wagon," related Jennings, who marked the dusty trail for days with bloody phlegm. "Even to this day [a third of a century later], that injury is still felt and I suffer from it."

Bones often snapped when a midnight ride turned ugly. As cattle hoofs thrashed shin oak in a dark run in Terry County, Texas, in 1898, trail boss B. A. Oden winced to a stinging rain and gigged his pony for the leaders. One moment he was riding in perfect form, and the next he was down, feeling the crush of his rolling horse.

"The boys found me and carried me to the wagon," remembered Oden, who broke two ribs. "I was so sore, they had to cut my slicker off."

When day broke, cowhands helped Oden on a horse, and the shaken waddy rode to the nearby NUN Ranch, where a woman treated his injuries. He managed to deliver the herd to Hereford, Texas, but his condition limited his effectiveness for months.

Like a soldier's war wounds, injuries could serve as a measure of a drover's obstinate courage, and any outfit with multiple mishaps in a stampede was to be admired. "Men . . . would do without sleep, go half-starved, and die before they would think of turning the herd plumb loose," Teddy Blue Abbott wrote in 1931.

J. T. Gardenhire and his fellow cowhands lived up to such a standard one autumn night in Texas when a horse shook its saddle and spooked a roundup herd of twelve hundred beeves. The waddies milled the herd again and again, only to watch an animal break through on each occasion and lead the cattle in another hazardous run. On until daybreak the cowhands struggled, chasing down the ornery herd a dozen times in testimony to their grit.

"One rider broke his leg in a fall from his horse, any number had sprains, and everybody had scratches all over them," noted Gardenhire. "One helluva night!"

Still, they could have counted themselves lucky, for a horse wreck among barreling cattle could have the gravest of consequences. James Childers, an Indian Territory cowboy, remembered two ZH waddies meeting such a death, while Texas cowhand Jap Adams witnessed similar tragedy when a shadowy rider overtook the leaders of a rampage. A crazed steer bumped the drover's horse, causing the pony to fall and crush the man to death. In another fatal incident, a cowpoke named Jack Owens disappeared during a series of stampedes between midnight and noon in the Keechie Creek valley of Texas. Searchers found his body and read a grim story of a rider taking a spill in the dark and fracturing his skull on a rock.

"We did not know where he was from, or where to find his folks, so we buried him there in the Keechie valley," remembered fellow drover Robert W. Keen.

Under extreme weather conditions, a rider felled by stampede might survive the moment only to die of exposure. As dusk neared on a zero-degree day in Wyoming about 1891, drovers felt the bite of whipping winds as they pushed five thousand beeves through the shadow of Chauvenet Mountain.

"I could see a great fog rising from the cattle that was coming from the heat of their bodies and breath," recounted George S. Stiers. "There was ice forming and settling on their backs. My eyelids and beard was taking on ice so fast that I could not hardly keep my peepers open."

The onslaught of a howling blizzard about nightfall added to the woes, and the drovers wisely forced a mill. Movement would generate heat, for either a single animal or thousands, and a mill's very nature decreed that outside cattle constantly work to the center where warmth was greatest.

Without warning, the herd broke to run with a clack of horns and rumble of hoofs. From the moment cowhands gave chase, they wanted only to keep the beeves together and let them run to exhaustion.

"The storm kept getting worse, and the critters kept running," continued Stiers. "It was one of them storms where if a fellow lost the herd, it would be a long chance of finding it again."

He clung to the herd throughout a one-hour run and on into daylight, when the storm relented enough for the drovers to realize that three cowhands were missing. One of the men, Texas Slim, dragged in that afternoon, but the fate of the others remained a mystery for months. After the spring snow melt, searchers discovered their decomposing remains. Whether the cowboys had died as a direct result of the stampede or had lost their bearings and succumbed to the elements, no one would ever know.

Anytime the ground suddenly fell away across a stampede rider's path, he had a one-way ticket to judgment. At the head of the Lampasas River in Texas one wet and frigid night, a thousand steers enticed a cowhand to the lead and straight into a lurking gully. His horse dropped violently, but momentum carried the man to the far bank and out of harm's way as steer after steer piled in the ditch behind. In another run, a black cowhand plummeted off a twenty-foot bluff twenty miles from San Antonio and had the presence of mind to shout a warning to trailing rider Robert William Little. Little, tearing through the night with his bronc at full gallop, still would have gone over, but his horse dug in its hoofs at precipice's edge.

"It never hurt the Negro and his horse very bad, but it could have killed them easy," Little recalled.

In a parallel catastrophe near the Solomon River in Kansas in 1880, two drovers chased down the leaders only to pitch headlong into a deep gully. As cattle began plunging over in their wake, one rider eased his fall by stepping off his horse, but the second rider, a black cowhand named Tom, tumbled hard. As the main herd veered, a third waddy, J. H. Hurley, pulled up at the rim and spotted Tom in the night.

"I thought at first he was hurt," Hurley remembered, "but I heard him sayin' something which was not his Sunday school lesson, and I knew he was all right."

Meanwhile, the storming herd swung again toward the gully, placing all three men in jeopardy.

"Negro Tom's curses turned to a prayer," recounted Hurley. "He yelled for me to help him out, but I knew I must turn the herd if possible or we'd all be trampled to death."

Shooting and shouting and spurring his horse, Hurley headed off the lead steer and turned the herd at the last instant.

A horse's innate night vision was often a stampede rider's greatest asset, but it also demanded vigilance against quick cuts and sudden stops. When Bud Fisher's charging pony burst upon a deep wash one stormy night, the animal planted its forelegs and threw the cowboy over its head. The next morning, searchers found him sitting in the arroyo and rolling a smoke.

"Why in hell are you sittin' there?" asked a rider.

"Well, I have no hankerin' for chuck, and walkin' is a trifle discomfortin' right now."

"What's agitatin' you?"

"Just my leg cracked," Fisher answered truthfully. "It tickles me when I walk, and that gets me to laughin' so hard that I have to sit down."

Occasionally, a drover's escape from mayhem almost defied belief. When big steers stampeded along the Smoky River in Kansas during an 1872 thunderstorm, Mark Withers touched spurs to his bronc to head them off. Racing at a dead gallop through swirling gloom, he never saw the sudden drop-off over his pony's ears until it was too late.

"He jumped and fell over the bank and landed on a part a little lower," Withers recounted in 1932. "The cattle came piling right on over my head, and not a single one hit me, except one kicked me on the hip."

Studying the scene by daylight, drovers counted ten or so cattle carcasses at the base of a drop deeper than the length of a lariat. Another twenty to twenty-five beeves had been crippled.

When a stampeding herd carried a rider into the murky depths of a river, he needed everything he could muster in the way of skill, luck, and Providence to see another sunrise. Otherwise, only a windswept grave would memorialize the fact that another young man had died a cowboy's death. A long-ago Arizona night racked by sky fire was the setting for one such tragedy, which took root when fifteen hundred cattle drew several Strayhorn outfit cowhands into a frenzied race. Storming the Pareco River, half the herd poured over the gloomy bank and lured four unaware riders into the turbulent waters.

"Immediately there was plenty of scrambling and floundering of men, cattle, and horses in the dark and rain," related eyewitness William Owens. "No one could see enough to do anything, and we just had to wait for daylight."

But two Strayhorn waddies had already seen their last sunrise, and all Owens could do by daylight was help commit the drowning victims to a deep grave on the bank of the Pareco and say a few heartfelt words.

"I requested the Lord to take them in because their hearts were pure as gold," Owens related. "While they were tough and cussed, all their acts were done in good faith. They were true to their fellow man, to their work, and to every trust."

With the introduction of barbed wire, another pitfall loomed for a horseman hurtling through the night. In a long-ago stampede near San Antonio, a galloping bronc struck a fence at an angle and threw its rider twenty feet across. In another barbed wire ambush, this one on the Texas plains in June 1904, the Grim Reaper almost branded Arch Sneed for the eternal range.

Before sunset that day, Sneed helped bed down twenty-seven hundred two-year-old steers just north of the Rock Island roundhouse at Dalhart. The cattle rested peacefully on into hard dark, but by the time Sneed rode out for guard duty about midnight, a storm and trouble had begun to brew. Within minutes, sky fire cracked, and the cattle were off like a covey of flushed quail.

Through a driving rain, Sneed pursued. "The cattle were running like an ocean," he recounted. "[I] was blinded by the flashes of lightning and the darkness. . . . I was following them as much by the noise as anything else."

Suddenly, to the lingering glare of a powerful bolt, the cowpuncher found himself within strides of the lead steers. Darkness again veiled the scene, and he brought his barreling horse abreast of the leaders only to crash violently into a barbed wire fence.

"My horse and I went plumb over," related Sneed, whose collision turned the herd and threw it into a mill. "When I tried to get up, I could not, and my right leg seemed numb."

To another bright flash, the injured man saw a nearby cow trail flowing with water and was overcome by abrupt thirst. Only as he crawled toward it did he discover the magnitude of his injury—wicked barbs had ripped through his doubled pants and high-top boots below the knee and had sliced his thigh to the bone. Blood oozed from the eight-inch gash.

He lifted his gaze to the lights of Dalhart flickering through the pouring rain and lost consciousness. After sunup, he awoke half-dead to find his lacerated pony standing nearby and wrangler Bud Farmer approaching on horseback. Farmer helped the injured cowpoke to the wagon and put him on a fresh mount, then led horse and rider to a Dalhart physician.

"He sewed up my leg with a needle like I had seen [used] to sew up sacks at a thresher," Sneed remembered. "All I could do was holler, as he had me strapped down and a two hundred-pound boy [sitting] on my head."

The most horrible of all deaths in a stampede was by trampling, a possibility every time a cowhand gigged a bronc after a herd gone mad. A single mistake could prove fatal, although rampaging beeves would generally split and run around an obstacle such as a downed rider if given time. But events came rapid-fire when cattle laid siege to the night, and a split second was sometimes the margin between life and death for a cowboy.

Getting caught afoot anywhere near a stampede was perilous. As W. E. Oglesby gathered firewood along Sycamore Creek on the outskirts of Fort Worth, he whirled to the thunder of hoofs and saw three thousand Four Six cattle bearing down on him like a speeding locomotive.

"The cattle were jumping twice their length with each leap," Oglesby recounted. "The riders were shooting their guns in the

Dust shrouding a Matador trail herd on a drive to Lubbock, Texas, in 1910. (E. E. Smith Collection, Nita Stewart Haley Memorial Library, Midland, Texas)

faces of the cattle and yelling their loudest but were not accomplishing a thing."

Pumping his legs desperately, Oglesby avoided the herd's path by the width of a hair. The cattle went on to assail a residential district and scatter the townspeople.

Every cowhand knew he could ill afford to go down amid a raging herd, where the earth rumbled and hoofs and horns flashed through billowing dust so thick that it could choke a man—if he lived long enough. When cattle bowled over one rider's mount in an 1873 run in Bexar County, Texas, the surging mass fortunately was too tightly packed to let the waddy fall through. Sprawled across tossing backbones and clashing horns, the cowhand rode the stampede a quarter-mile before escaping with only bruises.

If a drover did go down among runaways, any rescue attempt could result in two tragedies instead of one, yet no fellow rider with self-respect would just pass on by. As Wash Tankersley flanked a dark stampede near Sterling City, Texas, lightning flashed and he saw M. B. "Nub" Pulliam scrambling on hands and knees in the cauldron; a longhorn had felled his pony. Without hesitating, Tankersley touched spurs to his horse and forged through the rushing flood.

"Jump on, Nub!" he cried.

Pulliam lunged wildly for Tankersley's outstretched arm and clambered on behind. As Tankersley spurred his horse away and weaved a wild course through the onslaught, Pulliam was so intent on hanging on that he seized Tankersley by the ears and nearly pulled them off before they reached safety.

Downed riders sometimes eluded catastrophe by mere chance or benevolent grace. Such a beneficiary was William S. Knight, who intercepted a stampede in a black storm and rode stride for stride with the leaders. He wanted to crowd the beeves into turning, but as he took his horse in close, the renegades pushed back. When his horse veered to avoid a collision, the animal tripped and threw the cowboy fifteen feet into a night filled with dread.

"When I landed, I found myself in water about knee deep," Knight recounted. "I could hear the music of the tramping feet and clashing horns passing by."

After the cattle rushed away into sky fire, Knight waded out of the bog and felt his bronc nudge his back, a comforting moment in an hour so threatening.

In a New Mexico run instigated by Indians, horse wreck casualty Ben Davenport also caught a lucky break. As he and William A. Smith flanked the deafening herd to keep it bunched until a forward rider could force a mill, a hundred beeves managed to break away. The two men veered with the splinter group and quickly pushed to the front through gloom laced with rain. As they pressed close to the leaders to turn them back into the herd, Davenport's horse lurched into a narrow depression—right in the path of hundreds of flailing hoofs.

"I says to myself, Ben will get the eternal brand, sure," Smith recalled.

One after the other, however, the cattle jumped the ditch and spared the cradled cowhand.

In another providential fall, a cowboy survived a Texas stampede at the price of his horse. In a daring ride for point, Jacob Bennett and a second TC cowhand zigzagged between a storm of hides and horns and came up behind the leaders. As one steer weakened and a stronger one took its place, the second drover's bronc stumbled and fell just strides ahead of a crush of oncoming beeves. The horse broke its neck and died instantly, leaving the cowhand to face a more punishing death. With wisdom born of desperation, the cowboy threw himself behind the carcass and held his breath while an army of steers hurdled overhead.

Sometimes a downed rider formed his own barricade at the

smoking muzzle of a six-gun. Frank Smith, tossed into a boiling herd on a night lighted by sky fire, emptied his revolver at the brute-black shapes reeling toward him. He dropped enough beeves to make a crude fort that forced succeeding animals to veer left and right as they continued their frantic flight. Rowdy McGowan, desperate to throw up a breastwork in a separate incident, shot his horse and four or five charging cattle and survived his own brush with hell.

"You talk about a sick-looking waddy, Rowdy took the cake," remembered fellow cowhand J. C. Hess. "He didn't have a bit of color in his face."

Nevertheless, McGowan dusted himself off, saddled a fresh horse, and rejoined the chase—powerful testimony to "the stuff a cowpuncher had to be made of," reflected Hess.

However, it was up to T. N. McKinney and Eugene McCrohan to establish that a man afoot could turn a stampede or even split it from leaders to drags. Neither cowpoke set out to risk his life to prove a point; on the contrary, circumstances permitted no option but to stand firm and hope. McKinney showed his mettle when his horse went down in a badger hole in front of a thousand big steers in West Texas.

"The cattle split, and part of them went on one side of me and part on the other," he recounted.

McCrohan, victimized by a horse wreck at the head of another stampede, took nothing for granted when it came to the eyesight of the imminent horde. Ripping off his slicker, he whirled it overhead, inducing the beeves to dodge and storm harmlessly by.

Despite such accounts, forsaken graves from the Rio Grande north to Canada, from the Pecos west to the Pacific, silently affirm that tramplings did occur at times. To the bereaved, it was of no comfort that such deaths were freak occurrences. In another sense, though, tramplings were inevitable, considering all the potential scenarios in a hundred years of drives that dusted western trails.

A few charmed cowhands who offered themselves up for sacrifice lived to tell about it. When eight hundred big steers roared into a stormy Montana night in 1888, Teddy Blue Abbott's tired horse stumbled and fell. The impact snapped two of Abbott's ribs, but that was the least of his worries. Half-pinned under his wallowing mount, he felt the growing quake of the herd and threw out a hand to protect himself.

"They come so close that one steer struck me on the hand with his foot," Abbott wrote. "I carried the mark for years."

On another range pummeled by hoofs, the strike of a match almost cost a drover his life. When the flare panicked a drove and spurred it toward the high lonesome, William Riley Angermiller and a second rider doggedly pursued through a night ace-of-spades black. As the latter man overtook the renegades, a cow brute flattened his bronc.

"He was right in the way they were coming," remembered Angermiller. "When his horse fell, it turned the herd, but several trampled his horse and him too. It mashed him up pretty bad."

In the chaos of a stampede shrouded by darkness and rising dust, fatal tramplings seldom had eyewitnesses, and even a doomed man's cries were lost in the bedlam. Generally, only after the tumult subsided would drovers miss a rider, and even then the herd might be too volatile for the cowhands to organize an immediate search. When Abbott and his fellow waddies finally calmed a herd stampeded by rustlers in Indian Territory in 1879, they retraced the path of ruin and found the battered body of one of their own. In another tragic run one night, James Cape braved an electrical storm to save a herd, only to learn that another rider had met a gruesome end under the pile-driving hoofs.

Sometimes, such a death came on a cowboy's home range rather than along some faraway stretch of trail. In one case, a rider died in the crush of three thousand wild steers that W Ranch cowhands had rounded up along the Pecos River in Texas in prelude to a drive north.

"After the animals started to run, trying to stop the herd was useless," recalled William A. Preist, a W cowhand. "The old steers became furious and bowed their necks if a horse ran into their way."

The more extreme the conditions that contributed to a stampede, the greater the likelihood of accident, whether it be horse wreck or trampling. In Indian Territory one night, John H. Fuller of the CSJ outfit endured a storm that would have tested the courage of any stampede rider.

"The herd was a-going like something that broke out of the back door of hell," Fuller remembered. "The sky fire was shooting so fast that we could see the critters tolerably well. Those critters looked like a dark wave just going up and down, with fire hopping and skipping over their horns."

Astride a superb night horse, Fuller gained the lead and crowded the leaders, but even though his pony bit the beeves in the neck, the herd refused to veer. After brutal miles, the cattle finally ran themselves to exhaustion, but it wasn't until daylight that the drovers discovered a pair of waddies missing. They found "Red" sprawled with a broken leg and "Slim" trampled to death.

"No doubt," reflected Fuller, "his horse hit a hole and Slim took a spill among the running critters."

The only thing that distressed cowboys more than recovering a friend's trampled body was to realize their role in disrespecting his remains. When day broke after a night of stampede by five hundred cows on Nebraska's Blue River in 1876, cowhands found the body of a missing drover and his horse in a prairie dog town. The only thing recognizable was the handle of a six-gun.

"The horse's ribs was scraped bare of hide, and all the rest of horse and man was mashed into the ground as flat as a pancake," wrote Abbott, a fifteen-year-old witness to the mayhem. "The awful part of it was that we had milled them cattle over him all night, not knowing he was there."

The hoofs had been both deadly and profane, a synthesis unholy enough to haunt, but a cowhand nevertheless had something far more fiendish to fear.

Watery Graves

Ere long, the old trail drivers will have crossed over the river and staked their night horses on the other shore.

—W. C. Cochran, cowhand

An LS herd crossing the Canadian River in Texas in 1907. (E. E. Smith Collection, Nita Stewart Haley Memorial Library, Midland, Texas)

*I*n a profession teeming with hazard, a cowhand may have faced his greatest peril in crossing a swollen waterway, especially with a cattle herd. Not only did he invariably underestimate the power of rushing water—that most underrated of natural forces—but the very self-confidence and cautious trust in a horse that range life engendered in a cowboy worked against his survival. Only by experience could he truly gain respect for a river's sovereignty over rider and mount, but dead men never got second chances.

Across the West, cowpunchers confronted not only famous rivers such as the Red and the Platte, the Canadian and the Yellowstone, but nameless arroyos that could be bone dry one hour and foaming the next. Every channel offered its own demands, whether they involved depth or current, width or temperature, bank or bed, but the only constant about a waterway was its propensity for change. Nature could choke a docile stream to a trickle or transform it into a destructive force beyond the ken of a cowboy. Regardless, a cowhand might challenge it for the simplest of reasons: to get to the other side.

"Once more I can hear the trail boss tell someone to ride in to Doan's Store and see if there is any mail for the outfit," recalled a wistful Teddy Blue Abbott, who reached the Red River with northbound herds in the 1870s and 1880s. "And when he got back, we would ask how is the river, and he said 'She is up in the willows and running wild,' and the boss said, 'We will bust her tomorrow in spite of hell'—and we sure done her."

It was an attitude that could drive a cowboy either to succeed or to die. Still, few cowpokes were foolhardy, and most took precautions before riding into a river. A prudent cowhand might strip to his underwear, if not to his skin, and secure his garments and boots to saddle or wagon. His horse also required attention, and he would either remove the heavy saddle or loosen the cinches to permit the animal's lungs to expand easier and give it greater buoyancy.

The mechanics of crossing a cattle herd demanded not only knowledge of the river, but insight into bovine psychology. Mere time of day was a consideration, for a cow critter would not swim into a low-hanging sun with its blinding glare on the water. Hesitation, however, carried risk of its own, for drovers never knew when a sudden rise might deny passage indefinitely.

Even with the sun at its back, a herd generally resisted entering a river unless lured, a fact that often prompted punchers to start the remuda across first. Only then, perhaps, would the cattle take to the water, where mother cows would quickly assess the current and nudge their respective calves to their upstream sides. Cowhands also stayed busy, holding position around the herd to keep the beeves on course and to encourage the leaders to stay close to the remuda; if the gap widened to more than a hundred feet, the cattle might grow discouraged and turn back. As was the case in any phase of a drive, good point men were essential, but swing riders took on added importance in a rushing river. Swimming animals naturally veered downstream with the current, and only the presence of riders with boisterous voices and waving lassos might keep them headed across.

The most troublesome moment came when the cattle struck deep water, for their instinct was to reverse course and find firm footing again. To prevent a dangerous mill in midstream, it was crucial for riders to dart in quickly and keep the leaders on track for the far bank. Meanwhile, the cowboys' horses might be struggling themselves, lunging or floating on their sides rather than swimming. Overall, the massive scale of a crossing operation, in conjunction with the numerous dramas playing out against the dynamics of river and herd, could burn itself into a cowhand's memory like a hot iron in cowhide.

"To see two thousand head of cattle in the water at one time floundering and swimming, many with nothing but their heads and tails above water, is a sight one can never forget," observed W. B. Hancock, who pushed a drove north from Texas in 1879.

For men and animals alike, a waterway could be insidious, hiding its peril beneath a serene veil. Quicksand could not be seen, only felt, and by then it might be too late. Mire could be so tenacious that, as B. A. Oden said of the Pecos, a taut lariat might sooner yank another bend in the river than free a snared animal.

Regardless of the channel, no cowhand who nurtured a herd day and night could brace for the suffering displayed by hopelessly bogged wards. "It was terrible to hear them bawlin' and almost screamin' for help as they went down," reflected Ed Rawlings, who helped push four thousand XIT cattle into a Canadian River cursed by quicksand. "That was the saddest and most excitin' experience I've ever had with cattle."

In some cases, a rider was more than a disheartened onlooker, for through his very stirrups he could feel the suction's powerful grip on his battling horse. If he stayed astride, his added weight could seal both their fates, but abandoning his position would mean throwing himself at the mire's mercy. Depending on his response, he might either avert calamity or hasten it, but an informed decision required the kind of analytical thought for which no trapped cowboy had time. Subconsciously, he may have been aware of his horse's plight, his chances of rescue, the river's degree of treachery, and his own swimming ability, but instinct probably ruled his actions.

Sometimes a rider could engineer an escape by improvising. When drovers reached the Red River with a herd in 1874, they found it nearly a mile wide and raging, its foam-capped waves carrying drift of enormous size. Still, they had beeves to cross, and Joe

LS riders crossing Texas's Canadian River en route to the LIT range in 1907. (E. E. Smith Collection, Nita Stewart Haley Memorial Library, Midland, Texas)

Chapman took his horse into the turbulence in advance of the leaders. A quagmire in the shallows seized the diminutive paint, prompting the cowhand to climb off, strip, and divest the animal of saddle and bridle. Passing tack and belongings to another rider, Chapman swung up bareback and swam the paint across.

Anytime a cowboy dismounted under such circumstances, quicksand could take a death grip. Drover Mark Withers, scouting a Red River tributary by horseback, almost drowned in a mere six inches of water.

"As soon as I got in, the horse sunk, and every time he'd lunge, he'd go deeper," he related in 1932.

Desperate, Withers stepped off, only to experience firsthand the bog's ominous clutches. "Every time I stepped, I'd go down further," he lamented.

Fortunately, another rider was on hand to throw him a loop, which Withers quickly slipped over his torso. As the rider dragged him out, the cowhand left boots and spurs buried in the mire.

It was a fair trade for Withers's life, but sometimes a stream refused to negotiate. Near Seven Crook Ranch above Ogallala, Nebraska, Theodore Luce of Lockhart, Texas, met a gruesome end in the quicksands of the North Platte. It seemed impossible that anything good could spring from such a tragedy, yet in 1879 Samuel Houston Dunn took the loss of his friend as a warning to use the utmost caution in crossing a drove at Fort Laramie, Wyoming. When the last beef trudged up the far bank, Dunn quickly counted riders to make sure he wasn't consigning one more friend to the North Platte mire.

In a drive north from Mexico, Red River mud claimed a casualty of its own. When waddies pushed the remuda and seven hundred cattle into Doan's Crossing, swift currents swept the animals and rider Johnny Francis into a sheer bluff across the river. Underlying the water was vicelike quicksand that prevented escape. Horse piled upon horse, and beef upon beef, a frenzied log jam that churned the waters and dragged Francis into its clutches. His fellow cowboys never knew whether he perished by drowning or trampling, but either way he was no less dead.

Whether in shallows or deep water, a rider needed to bear in mind that every bronc had its limitations. A horse plunging into its first river might lunge instead of swim, while even an experienced pony might yield to the current rather than strike out for the far bank. When one such roan refused to swim the Red River in 1874, drovers had no choice but to ferry the animal across.

"He would only turn up on his side, curl his tail, and float back to the bank," remembered Chapman.

With horses prone to such idiosyncrasies, any cowhand too dependent on his mount could wind up in a watery grave. No matter his pony's proficiency on land, a wise cowhand needed to temper trust with caution as he studied a river between his animal's ears. Wisdom, however, often came only after a long apprenticeship with stubbornness.

As cowhands readied to shove a drove into the Canadian in 1880, the trail boss encouraged seventeen-year-old Jack Price Borland to change horses.

"The one you're riding won't swim," he warned.

Nevertheless, the cocky kid wouldn't listen. "Who ever heard of a horse that wouldn't swim?" Borland mused.

He brashly proceeded to take the horse into the swirling waters, only to fight for his life when the bronc rolled on its side and drifted downstream.

"One of the boys roped him and pulled him out, saving my gear and the horse," Borland recalled. "I found out that all horses couldn't swim."

No one alerted E. M. "Mac" Storey to his mount's shortcomings as he studied a Washita River tributary in present-day Oklahoma in 1871, but the result was the same; when he jumped his horse into the stream, the animal surrendered to the flow. Luckily, Storey floated the bronc to a sandbar across the channel, but he lost his saddlebags and clothes.

Anytime a rider couldn't swim, he could only trust in his fragile aura of invincibility and forge into a channel—risky business considering how little he might know of his bronc's water skills. Mac Stewart, returning from a drive to Kansas with three hundred dollars in his saddle, nearly drowned when his pony rolled with him in the surging Red River. A fellow cowhand, E. A. "Berry" Robuck, saved the struggling man and joined in a daring recovery of his money.

On a northbound drive originating in Mexico, another cowhand deficient in swimming pulled rein at the Rio Grande eight miles up-

Vaqueros pushing a John R. Blocker herd across the Rio Grande at Langtry, Texas, in 1914. (E. E. Smith Collection, Nita Stewart Haley Memorial Library, Midland, Texas)

stream of Eagle Pass, Texas. In deference to the swift waters, the trail boss restricted the vaquero to the bank, where he did his part by goading the beeves into the channel. After the last beef reached Texas soil, another Mexican cowboy shouted across and encouraged the vaquero to join him in town. Ignoring the warnings of others, the vaquero urged his bronc into the current.

"It carried him, horse and all, right on down the river," related S. H. Blalock. "The old horse wouldn't swim, either, he just sort of floated down and the Mexican sitting on top of him."

As the second Mexican kicked his pony into desperate flight along the bank and came abreast, the vaquero lost his grip. His frantic cries were still echoing when he vanished in the waters. Days later, searchers recovered his body near a bridge that could have given the vaquero safe passage.

Even if a horse was a swimmer, it might lack the endurance to transport a waddy across a demanding stream. The mile-wide Missouri River was so daunting that only four of forty saddle animals in one trail outfit crossed on their own; the others would swim a short distance and turn on their sides. In an extraordinary move, drovers crossed the ponies in pairs and paddled a boat alongside in order to hold the animals' heads above water.

If a swimming horse weakened with a rider astride, the cowboy might take extreme measures to lessen the animal's burden. When William Walter Brady returned alone from a drive and plunged his horse into the flooded Trinity River in Texas, a powerful current struck his pony broadside. Swept downstream, the animal began to fade, even as the alarmed cowhand shed boots and heavy accoutrements.

"By the time we reached the middle of the water, I had thrown my food away and was really worried," Brady recalled.

Suddenly he heard the shout of an elderly hog farmer on the bank. "Let him have his head! Get off and hold to his tail!"

In a rare case of a cowboy deferring to a farmer in a matter of horsemanship, Brady slid off and seized the bronc's tail. Through turbid waters and surging currents, he clung desperately as the reinvigorated animal angled for the muddy bank.

"Man! Was I a sight when I came out of the water," Brady remembered. "No shoes, no hat, saddle, clothes, or nothing."

Fortunately, the farmer outfitted the waddy with worn shoes and a hat for the last leg of his journey.

Trading a position astride a horse for a grip on its tail was often effective in staving off disaster. When exhaustion threatened Babe Moye's Spanish mount in the Red River in 1872, the drover eased off the pony's hindquarters, found a hold, and let the unburdened animal pull him across. W. B. Hancock, straddling a fatigued horse in the out-of-bank Canadian, took time to unbridle his animal before similarly grasping the appendage.

Sometimes, a pony's tail was a veritable lifeline to a drowning cowboy. As Jim Newton waded his horse across the South Platte in Nebraska in 1879, the animal stepped into deep water and dragged him under. Swept from the saddle, Newton caught his foot in his lariat and struggled in the dark waters. He broke free just in time to grasp the horse's tail and let the animal pull him to safety.

In an 1884 incident, a black drover managed to reach a sandbar in the middle of the flooded Canadian after his exhausted horse succumbed. S. B. Brite swam his pony to the stranded man and towed him across via the animal's tail.

"The Negro thanked me and said that horse's tail was just like the 'hand of Providence,'" Brite related.

A bovine's tail, as well, could deliver a cowhand from the depths. When Gus Staples reached the Red River with a northbound drove in 1876, he found the scowling barrier intimidating. "It was either turn back or grab an old cow by the tail and let her pull me across," he wrote, "so I tailed her and reached the other side safely."

Sometimes, a tiring horse and an unforgiving current conspired to doom a rider. In 1892, the foreman of the N Bar N drowned when the North Platte claimed his spent bronc, and a similar fate befell a drover astride a bobtailed horse in the Smoky River in Kansas in 1869.

"[The drover] said if my little mule could swim the river, 'Old Bob' could swim it," related J. M. Cowley.

Nevertheless, the stamina of the bobtailed bronc was inferior to the mule's, and it sank with its rider. Cowley threw a desperate loop, but the man failed to catch it and disappeared in the waters.

Another peril to a cowpoke was the paralyzing shock of cold water. When Teddy Blue Abbott reached the Yellowstone River in Montana with a drove, he found the channel fringed by ice. Nevertheless, he safely crossed on a big Oregon horse that, even with the burden of a rider, swam high enough in the water to keep the saddle dry. Meanwhile, drovers who straddled Texas ponies endured a frigid ordeal, for the animals kept only their heads above water.

"The damned little stinkers will keep reaching for the bottom with their hind feet, so it's all you can do to keep from being drowned off their backs," wrote Abbott.

When the icy flow struck one such rider in Abbott's outfit, he reflexively cried out and dived over his bronc's head. On his own in unbearable cold, he might have drowned if he hadn't seized a swimming beef by the tail.

"He never let go until the steer dragged him halfway up the bank and . . . took all the skin off his knees," remembered Abbott.

In 1877, a furious hailstorm pounded naked drovers as they started across the deluged North Canadian with a herd. Soon the water rushed white, visual evidence of a water temperature drop so drastic that it drove cowhands and beeves to the nearest land. A single rider reached the far bank with half the drove, but now he was stranded without clothes and out of earshot. Although his companions recognized his susceptibility to hypothermia, river conditions thwarted their repeated attempts to deliver him clothes.

"The water was so cold that [neither] horse nor man could endure it," remembered Jerry M. Nance. "In trying to cross over, several of them came near drowning and were forced to turn back."

With a cowboy's resourcefulness, the naked cowhand wrapped himself in a saddle blanket and weathered the night. By morning, the river's temperature was back to normal, and drovers and animals again had passage.

In rushing water, a rider always had to prepare for the unexpected. Breakers, for example, might sweep him off his horse and cast him to the whims of powerful undercurrents. The Yellowstone was notorious for its undertow, but waterways such as the Trinity in Texas could drown just as surely if a rider lost his hold. As drovers waited for a Trinity rise to subside in the 1870s, the cook's assistant risked the channel to retrieve a yearling. Unable to cling to his mule, he vanished in the torrent. When the tide waned, cowhands discovered his body dangling by a boot caught in a tree fork—a grisly monument to a river's sovereignty.

In 1873, the white-capped Red River almost claimed Tony Williams as he pointed a herd across. Whisked from his mule by oppressive waves, he stayed alive only by clutching a steer's tail.

Drover Leo Tucker, who sometimes swam a horse across the Red thirteen times in a single day, almost met his demise in a small creek near St. Joe, Missouri, in 1875. Asleep when roaring floodwaters stampeded the herd, he awoke with a start, jumped on his bronc, and started across to join the chase. But the current was stronger than his grip, and in moments he was adrift. Even after another cowboy roped and dragged the half-drowned man to shore, his survival was doubtful. Cowhands finally resuscitated him, but he remained unconscious for hours.

Faced with such consequences, a rider traversing an unyielding tide needed to concentrate all his energies toward staying with his bronc. Drover J. C. Hess, swimming his horse across a river at near-flood stage, casually scooted off the animal's hindquarters and clasped its tail, only to slip free. As the current bore him downstream, Hess could only float on his back and hope for deliverance. A waddy wearing a neckerchief dived in and swam to Hess, who held to the bandanna as his rescuer towed him to safety.

No matter the reason a horse and rider separated, the puncher was vulnerable to an inadvertent hoof as the animal struggled. In the Arkansas River in June 1872, a loosed rider took a stunning blow and would have drowned if an onlooker hadn't swum to his aid. Two years later in the Red River, a bronc pawed a drover named Barkley, necessitating another bold rescue.

But a cowhand couldn't dwell on a single hazard when a turbulent stream offered so many. The terrific force of surging driftwood, for example, could cut a rider from his horse quicker than anything. When John Young arrived at the Colorado River in Texas with a drove in 1880, he found a deluge four hundred yards wide. He swam his horse to midstream without incident, then a barreling timber bowled him over. Swamped and detached from his bronc, the injured cowboy bested the dark waters and surfaced, only to find his animal out of reach. He struck out for shore, but drifted hundreds of yards downstream before Gus Claire overtook him on a horse carried by the same current.

"As he passed by," Young related, "I caught the horse by the tail, when suddenly we got into a swift eddy, which carried us under a bluff, where we could not land."

With one cowboy astride and a second in tow, the pony finally escaped the eddy and gained the far bank.

Even for a man ashore, driftwood could be hazardous. In 1871, five cowboys bound for Dodge City found the rampaging Washita impassable and set about securing materials for a raft. When Billie Gray roped a large tree as it hurtled downstream, the log's momentum yanked him into the river. Unable to swim, the cowhand bobbed and tumbled in the foam but managed to seize a sudden lariat from shore.

The roper, E. M. "Mac" Storey, believed Gray had missed the throw and dived in to save him. Storey still gripped his lariat, and he felt a tug even before he popped up to see Gray at the other end. As the river's powerful drive carried Storey under a willow, he grabbed a pliant limb. Gray, working against pouring tons of water, navigated the tide by rope and caught Storey by the neck, momentarily submerging them both. Storey kept his hold on the willow, however, and the cowhands soon made their way to the bank.

With a channel swarming with so many threats, wisdom wasn't always enough to keep a cowboy alive, but foolhardiness could virtually guarantee a trip over the great divide. As a pair of saddle tramps pulled rein at the bank-full Cimarron in Indian Territory in 1874, they found northbound drovers waiting for the swell to subside. The drovers urged them to be patient, but the tramps stubbornly jumped their horses into the swirling currents. By midriver, they were in serious trouble.

"They began yelling for us to come and help them out," remembered drover Babe Moye.

But the saddle bums were beyond the reach of a lariat, and all anyone could do was watch them die.

Of the many pitfalls in a waterway, a mill was the deadliest, for river hydraulics and seething cattle interacted to spawn a maelstrom of incredible force. A beef was no longer an individual but a cog in a churning machine that impeded the channel's very flow. Every time leaders reached deep water and wanted to retreat, a mill was a threat; if cowhands allowed the herd to turn back in on itself, they were sure to face an aqueous tornado with a life of its own.

"The first thing you know [the cattle] will start to jump up and ride one another, trying to climb out, and down they will go," reflected Teddy Blue Abbott.

Faced with losing a great many cattle, cowhands took desperate measures to end such tumult.

"We had to take our clothes off, ride our horses out to the middle, and turn the leader right," Tom McClure said of a mill in the South Canadian. "[They were] packed so close together that a man could almost have walked from one side to the other on their backs."

When a drove milled in the Red River on June 8, 1871, owner W. M. Todd implored twenty-two-year-old W. B. Foster to save his herd, setting the stage for an act of daring equal to any in the annals of trail driving. Stripping to his underwear, Foster plunged his bronc into the swollen stream and urged it toward the upheaval. At the mill's fringe, he abandoned the horse, leaped atop the stirring backbones, and weaved through a pitchfork of horns.

"[Cattle] were so jammed together that it was like walking on a raft of logs," Foster recalled.

Gambling that the mass wouldn't part and swallow him, Foster worked his way to the largest steer, straddled it, and turned the animal toward the far bank. As the steer broke from the mill, the other mossy-horns followed. Still, Foster was astride a wild steer, no place to be once the beef reached firm footing. As the bovine neared shore, the waddy eased into the water and drifted downstream to his horse.

It was a peaceful end to a dangerous situation, but sometimes a mill had tragic results. When a point rider got caught up in such a cauldron in the flooded Colorado near La Grange, Texas, in 1880, he disappeared amid the frenzied beeves and thrashing water. It was the last time anyone saw him alive; two days later, his bloated corpse surfaced four hundred yards downriver.

As challenging an enemy as a waterway could be, however, a cowboy's most cunning adversary sometimes lurked in his very shadow.

Flying Fists and Gun Smoke

I have not done the good I might have done, but pray that my follies
and mistakes may be forgiven and forgotten.

—James H. Baker, cowhand

*M*an was the West's greatest predator.

Volatile, impatient, impulsive, scheming—any of
these might describe the person driven to violence
by anger, circumstance, or a warrior mentality. Whether bearing the
trappings of cowhand or Indian, he could draw blood in the flash
of a fist, the twitch of a trigger finger, the twang of a bow string. In
his own mind, he may have meted out justice or retribution, or satisfied the demands of a warrior society, but regardless he was a danger with which to reckon.

Any type of violence between cowhands was usually frowned
upon by cattle outfits, which sometimes were quick to make exam-
ples of guilty parties.

"You was fired at the JAs for three things, and that was for
drinking and fighting and gambling," remembered Fish Wilson,
who rode for the Texas Panhandle outfit in the 1940s.

"If you couldn't get along with your fellow workers, why, they
didn't want you," elaborated Fred McClellan, another Southwestern hand.

Still, when tempers flared, cowboys didn't always keep job security in mind, even if they worked for outfits with strict rules of conduct.

"You get a bunch together, and nearly always there'll be somebody that's a little out of line," observed Green Mankin, who punched cows in the Ozona country of Texas in the 1920s and 1930s.

"Oh, man, I tell you, we had lots of fights," added Leonard Hernandez, another Texas cowboy of the 1920s. "Sometimes we'd even put out the fire, rolling in the ashes. You can't count the cuts I got on my head."

Occasionally, a waddy tested the mettle of a newcomer by goading him into a fight, although wisdom demanded careful preliminary assessment of a stranger's physical abilities. When six-foot, four-inch Buck McCain hired on with the Hoover Ranch near Ozona prior to the Great Depression, an ornery cowhand took an immediate dislike to him.

"I think I'll just whip him," the cowhand confided to Mankin.

Mankin studied the massive stranger, whose legs were long enough to wrap around even the stoutest horse. "I think you better look at him a second time," he urged.

Nevertheless, the cowhand proceeded to pick a fight with McCain.

"Man! There wasn't no fight to it," Mankin recalled many years later. "McCain hit the ol' boy one time, and he folded up like a chair."

McCain soon proved to be a contradiction in terms: likable yet always ready with fists worthy of a barnstorming pugilist.

"It was in his blood—he'd rather fight than to do anything else," reflected Mankin, whose own fighting instincts were the stuff of Texas legend. Only average sized at one hundred sixty pounds, Mankin was a friend of McCain's and never tangled with him, but the David-and-Goliath matchup would have been intriguing.

Green Mankin, Gaston Boykin, and Ted Powers in Texas in 1926. (Photo courtesy of Gaston Boykin)

"Mankin was the toughest guy I've ever known," testified Gaston Boykin, a one-time cowhand who served as a Texas sheriff for twenty-eight years. "Good fellow but terrible high-tempered. If you made him mad, you got some trouble, I don't care how many was on the other side. And the more there were, the worse he was."

Another Ozona cowpuncher, Ted Powers, concurred: "It would've took a prizefighter to whip him. Mankin trained all time just like a prizefighter and wrestler. He worked out on me a lot. He jogged and ran; he wouldn't smoke; he wouldn't drink coffee even. And he sure didn't drink whiskey."

One day at a lower Pecos bunkhouse, unsuspecting Carl Pettit got riled at Mankin and decided to confront him. When Mankin entered the bathroom, Pettit barged in and locked the door.

"Green liked to tore that bathroom down with him," related Powers. "Pettit was hollerin', 'Green, let's quit!' So they opened the door and separated them."

When Mankin and Powers ventured to Globe, Arizona, in the late 1920s, the cowpokes entered a boot shop and found the cobbler huge and muscled.

"What part of Texas you boys from?" asked the cobbler.

"Ozona," Mankin replied.

"Oughta be a lot of good people down there," said the cobbler.

"What do you mean?"

"Well," snarled the man, "there's so many sorry SOBs here from there, if there's any left, they oughta be all right."

Mankin took it for the insult it was. He bellowed a challenge, and the bear-of-a-cobbler grinned and pulled off his apron.

"Ol' Green went to runnin' at him just as hard as he could," related Boykin. "That ol' boy hit him, and Green went fifteen feet. He got up and here he come back, just as hard as he could run. Fellow hit him again—end over end he went."

After the third or fourth knockdown, Mankin employed a different tactic.

"He started runnin' circles around the fellow," Boykin continued. "He'd run in and jump back—he was fast as lightning."

Suddenly Mankin drove a crushing fist into the cobbler's Adam's apple and felled him in a corner.

"Green liked to beat him to death," noted Boykin. "Took two cops to get him off of him."

But even in battle, Mankin had a prizefighter's honor. "He'd fight a fellow and get up and shake hands and go on and be friends," related Powers.

Such an attitude was not uncommon among cowhands, who might wipe away blood and grudges at the same time. On a three-month drive from the Midland country of Texas north in 1930, point rider Slim Vines chastised a young drover named Cruise for abandoning drag and disrupting the lead cattle. After the herd reached a ranch near Whiteface, the bad blood between the two escalated into carefully measured violence. When they dismounted and faced one another, Vines drew back a fist, but Cruise hesitated.

"Wait a minute now—get those spurs and leggings off," urged Cruise. "We want to have a fair fight. If you can whip me, all right. If you can't, why, I'm gonna whip you."

Vines obliged, and as soon as they shed their accoutrements, Cruise charged and jutted out his chin.

"I hit him on the side of the ear and just flattened it," Vines recalled six decades later. "After a lick or two, I hit him on the nose and made it bleed. We fought for thirty minutes, until we gave completely out. I was exhausted. My lungs was burnin', and I turned both of my thumbs back, out of place. I was afraid that guy never would give up. I was afraid to, afraid he wouldn't stop."

Finally, Cruise peeled himself off the ground and extended a hand of friendship. "Well," he admitted as Vines accepted his clasp, "I didn't think you could do it, but you whipped me. Let's just don't hold that against each other."

"If that's the way you want it," agreed Vines.

Although neither cowhand retained ill feelings, Vines couldn't shrug off his dislocated thumbs so easily; for weeks, he couldn't cinch a saddle or grip his reins.

"I'd ride holding my reins with my thumbs sticking up," he remembered. "The boys got to mocking me; they'd ride by me and stick their own thumbs up."

Anytime an altercation involved weapons, the principals were unlikely to walk away so amicably. In a Spade wagon camp in Texas one morning, the cook's natural contrariness turned to rage when Homer Martin was late to the serving line. The cook seized a pot hook and started after him, but Martin jerked out a knife and sent the man scurrying.

In the lower Pecos country in the 1920s, a pair of cowboys locked horns in another fray that could have turned deadly. The incident began when wagon boss George Atkins dispatched Arch Cook and young Ted Powers to gather horses. Cook, however, convinced Powers to accompany him to a still, where cowhands Bill DeLong and Carl Cooper were bottling prohibition beer.

When Powers and Cook failed to show up with the broncs, Atkins rode in search and found the two waddies more concerned with home brew than horses. By now, the beer had flowed freely, emboldening all four cowpokes. When Atkins condemned Powers for shirking his duty, the older cowhands rose to his defense and a free-for-all erupted, culminating in a clash between Cooper and DeLong.

"DeLong could sure fight, good boxer," Powers related. "He whipped ol' Cooper. Cooper run backwards and quit, and he reached and got a long ol' knife that he kept sharp as a razor."

Suddenly, DeLong drew his own knife. "Come on!" he cried. "We'll just lock hands and cut it out!"

His challenge was enough to deter Cooper, who turned and fled.

As dangerous as a knife was, a club could be even more effective, for it could crush a man's skull in a single blow. Unfortunately, few cowhands appreciated its deadliness, leading to incidents of unintended manslaughter such as that in east-central Colorado in June 1878. As Samuel Caldwell Jr. sat in a line shack on the MacMillan spread that stormy day, he saw a cattle herd appear over a hill and two riders approach with a wagon.

"They said they were in bad luck this time, as they had a dead man in the wagon and that he had been killed by one of his companions," he wrote his mother in Boston.

Caldwell soon pieced together the details: The two young men had been friends from the same Missouri town, and as the trail outfit had broken camp that morning, they had begun to quarrel. One had jumped off his horse, seized a billet of wood, and struck his friend in the head, stunning him. When the victim had regained consciousness, cowhands had helped him into the wagon and offered to take him to Hugo for medical attention. The injured man had declined, however, citing his preference to accompany the cowhands to their home ranch. When they had checked on him a few hours later, they had found him dead.

"I had never seen the dead man," Caldwell wrote, "but his assailant I had met several times and liked him because he was overflowing with animal spirits and always singing, laughing, and talking."

Now, though, as the men unloaded the body at the line-shack door, the young cowhand was subdued.

"I had to step over it in going in and out in my preparations for supper," Caldwell recalled. "The young murderer came in and made a pretense of eating while the rain dripped coldly on his victim not twenty feet away and the lightning flashed and thunder rattled as if in reprobation of the wicked deed."

Later that day, the assailant rode away alone, supposedly to give himself up.

"He didn't care for himself, but he knew it would kill the mothers of both," noted Caldwell. "In gratifying a momentary fit of temper, he has brought sorrow and disgrace on two families, and on himself a burden of shame and remorse that a lifelong repentance cannot lift."

As cowardly and brutal as the assailant's act had been, it paled before that displayed on the trail to Kansas one night in 1873. As John W. Piree, his half brother Thomas Grayson, Tom Adams, and another drover named Utz curled peacefully in their bedrolls, a Mexican brandishing a club skulked into camp.

"[He] was a much trusted work hand in our neighborhood and had gone along with the outfit," noted E. M. Edwards, Piree's nephew by marriage.

Unaccountably, the Mexican bludgeoned all four men in the head as they slept. Fleeing, the perpetrator reportedly escaped into Mexico and disappeared into history, but he had already guaranteed himself a dark page in trail driving annals. Grayson died within hours and Piree two days later, and even though the other victims survived, Adams would always be disfigured.

Sometimes a cowboy paid an immediate price for lifting a cudgel. At a Cross-L camp along Currumpaw Creek near Des Moines, New Mexico, a cowpuncher named Brown grabbed a pan and dish rag from the chuck box to wash his sore-backed horse. In doing so, he violated an unwritten rule of a cow camp, for no self-respecting cook would let a cowhand trespass on his private domain. The Cross-L cook, Magill, not only railed about the transgression, but rushed after the cowhand. When Brown responded by threatening him with a single tree, the cook drew a firearm and plugged Brown through the nose. From that day forward, the Cross-L camp was known as "Dish Rag."

In angry hands, an ax could be far more lethal than a club, reason enough to take its menace seriously. On an 1871 drive to Kansas, another surly camp cook brandished an ax before the muzzle of a cowhand's cocked revolver. If trail boss W. F. Burks hadn't ridden up and ended the standoff, blood almost certainly would have been shed.

Not that any perpetrator cared, but the aftermath of a death by hacking made for a horrid scene. As Frank Yeary and another cow-

A cowboy displaying appropriate use of an ax on the OR Ranch in Arizona in 1909.
(E. E. Smith Collection, Nita Stewart Haley Memorial Library, Midland, Texas)

boy rode the Figure Five range near Forsan, Texas, in the late 1930s or early 1940s, they found sheep scattered far and wide—an unusual development, considering a shepherd's dedication to keeping his flock bunched as a precaution against predators.

"We couldn't figure what in the Sam Hill was goin' wrong," Yeary remembered.

Riding to the sheep camp, they made a grisly discovery. "Somebody had knocked the sheepherder in the head with an ax and killed him," Yeary related. "He was layin' there by the wagon. He'd been dead for two or three days. I won't never forget that day."

The murder was never solved.

A cowboy's weapon of preference was a firearm—a six-shooter maybe, or a thirty-thirty rifle. Era largely dictated how commonplace they were in a cowboy's life, and by the late 1800s it was generally illegal for a man to carry a pistol on his person. The wilder the country, however, the longer the practice remained acceptable, and lawmen in sparsely settled regions tolerated the custom well into the twentieth century.

Although a six-shooter in a rider's belt or a Winchester on his saddle could catch a limb or stray loop, a firearm could also dispense of rattlers or predators and protect a cowpoke from enraged bulls or crazed broncs. Its discharge could also fell game in an emergency or serve as a signal for help, while no prudent cowhand dared enter Indian or outlaw country without the security of its muzzle. Prior to the mid-1880s, a cowboy might have all of these reasons to keep a six-gun handy, but man was the greatest threat.

"'When God made man, He made him unequal in size,'" quoted Andre Jorgenson Anderson, who established a gun shop in Fort Worth in 1877. "'Later He saw His mistake, and to rectify His error, he had a man named Colt make pistols.'"

Indeed, the first thing a frontier cowhand did upon awakening was buckle on his six-shooter. "It was just as natural for a man to do that as it was for him to put on his hat," noted G. W. Roberson, who punched cattle in Texas and New Mexico.

"In those days, the six-shooter was a part of a man's dress the same as his pants were," agreed Earnest Cook, who was born in 1881. "No one would think of going out without his gun on."

Moreover, a firearm sometimes constituted the only law, albeit a jurisprudence interpreted solely by the man behind the trigger. Even on outfits such as the Texas Panhandle's XIT, which encouraged hands to restrict their firearms to the chuck box, revolvers had a way of staying within arm's reach.

"You might not think there was a six-shooter in camp, but let a fuss start and in two minutes every mother's son of them would have a gun on," noted XIT cowhand C. R. Smith.

Assuredly, unless a cowboy was willing to swap lead, he needed to throw his gun away and avoid disagreements, for many cow-hands knew no other way to fight.

"If God Almighty'd wanted me to fight like a dog," wrote Teddy Blue Abbott, "he'd have given me long teeth and claws."

But a firearm could also serve as a peacemaker, deterring trouble before it started.

"Son, why you carry that gun?" someone once asked Thomas Henderson, who packed a forty-five automatic in the Big Bend of Texas from age twelve in 1920. "You afraid of somebody?"

"Hell, no, I'm not afraid of anybody," Henderson replied. "I'm afraid of *everybody*. If you've got a gun people won't mess with you."

Looking back in 1990 from the perspective of eighty-one years, Henderson reaffirmed the wisdom of his practice.

"It kept me out of a lot of trouble, just having a gun," he observed.

By the 1910s, possession of a six-shooter was often more of a rite of passage than a necessity, but that was reason enough for some young cowboys.

"Ninety percent of us carried a pistol," recalled Joe Lambert, who rode the Texas range before giving up the profession in 1919. "We didn't think we was grown till we got to where we could carry a pistol and roll and light a Bull Durham cigarette with the horse a-trottin'."

Lonnie Griffith, who took up cowboying on a West Texas spread in 1915, learned his proficiency with firearms from his stepfather.

"He could ride a horse at full tilt and roll a tin can in front of him six shots out of six with a Colt forty-five," he remembered.

On into the 1920s in Arizona, where the Old West was making its last stand, cowboys routinely rode into town with their revolvers in plain sight.

"Everybody packed a gun then," recalled Tom Blasingame, who

Tom Blasingame with calf in tow in the 1920s. (J. Evetts Haley Collection, Nita Stewart Haley Memorial Library, Midland, Texas)

worked for the Double Circle, Chiricahua, and two other Arizona ranches. "That was just that kind of country. The sheriff didn't worry about it—if you didn't kill nobody, he didn't bother you."

With such a prevalence of firepower throughout the West at times, trouble was sure to break out. Often, the mere display of a weapon spoke with the same force as its report, as Slim Vines could attest after an incident on the Open A south of Midland, Texas, in the late 1920s or early 1930s. After Vines trained a brown horse for the outfit, ranch owner O. P. Jones presented him with the animal. Soon afterward, though, the foreman transferred Vines to a sister spread and the cowhand left the bronc behind. When Vines returned to pick up several horses, including the brown, he came face to face with a cowhand named Hogan, a tough ex–border patrolman with a bad reputation. In his days riding the Rio Grande, Hogan reportedly had killed a Mexican national without cause.

"I come over here to get some horses," Vines told him.

"What horses you gonna get?" snarled Hogan. He slung back his coat, revealing a pistol. "You're not gettin' that brown horse."

"But old man Jones gave me that horse," explained Vines.

"I said you wasn't gettin' him."

Studying the pistol, Vines knew better than to press the issue. He rode away, counting himself lucky to be alive.

Although Hogan's threat was unjustified, certain situations demanded a drawn gun. Around the XIT's Trujillo line shack in the Texas Panhandle, for example, outlaws were so common that no cowhand dared go outside unarmed.

"I went to Trujillo one night, rode up and called, and thought the man recognized me," related Ira Aten of the XIT. "I walked in the door and White, who was there, had a six-shooter sticking in my belly."

Aten didn't hold it against the man, for his own practice was to distrust any stranger who rode up at night. However, to pull a gun unjustly was a serious offense in a cowboy's mind, and he might sacrifice his very job to stand by his convictions.

After 7D drovers bedded down a herd on a West Texas drive about 1926, they paid a visit to a nearby bootlegger and returned with whiskey. Camp soon grew lively, with plenty of augering, singing, and mischief.

"One would go to bed, and some of the other boys would roll him out—just playing, nobody getting mad," recalled Douglas Poage, a Bar S "stray man" temporarily assigned to the 7D.

When a prankster entered one man's tent, however, the occupant was in no mood for deviltry and pulled a gun. The prankster, more angry than afraid, wrenched the weapon from the man and dragged him from the tent.

"He picked him up by his feet and just whipped the ground with him, then beat on him awhile," related Poage. "They finally pulled him off."

The next morning, the boss fired the assailant, setting off a chain reaction that saw every 7D drover quit in protest.

Fortunately, no shots had been fired in the incident, but gunplay had been only a muscle twitch away—a matter that sometimes demanded harsh punishment in the code of the West. Cattleman Charles Goodnight, a former Texas Ranger as tough as saddle leather, required new hands to commit to a contract that spelled out the consequences if such action led to an unjustified killing.

"If a man used a gun," Goodnight flatly stated, "he was to be hung."

Although a death sentence required an improvised trial by a defendant's peers, the mere suggestion of a necktie party was enough to make cowhands across the West reconsider even as they yanked out their revolvers. One alternative to squeezing the trigger was to wield the weapon like a club. Headed north to Kansas with a herd in 1869, two drovers got into an altercation that ended when one "struck the other over the head with a six-shooter," James H. Baker wrote in his diary on August 29. More than a generation later in 1914, rancher Riley Smith drove up to a chuck wagon in the Big Bend of Texas and began passing around a bottle of booze. After a few white cowhands took sips, Smith extended the bottle to Juan Silvas, a six-foot, three-inch vaquero with enviable cowboying skills.

"Oh man, he was fork-ed; he could sure ride a bronc," recalled Thomas Henderson, who was at the wagon that morning.

When Smith asked Silvas if he wanted a drink, the vaquero replied with a simple "No." Smith, half-drunk and a troublemaker, seized the opportunity to castigate the Mexican.

"You black SOB, you tell me 'No, sir!'" he snapped.

Henderson's father quickly spoke up. "Riley, he don't know how to speak English. He come from across the river."

"I don't give a damn where he come from—he's gonna say 'No, sir' to me!"

Jerking out his gun, Smith bludgeoned the Mexican in the face.

"The next lick was my daddy's fist on the side of Riley's damn jaw," Henderson related three-quarters of a century later. "He knocked him on his rear and got that gun."

In an incident with similar racial overtones on a drive up from Texas in 1879, another cowhand defended a beleaguered victim. The episode began when Ira Olive tried to provoke a black cowhand named Kelly into drawing a revolver so he could kill him. When a good cussing didn't work, Olive struck him in the mouth with a gun and knocked out a couple of teeth.

"I told him [Olive] if he hit that boy again I would shoot his damn eyes out," wrote Teddy Blue Abbott.

There was no defense for Olive's actions, but the pressures of a day-and-night drive across brutal country for relentless months could put any cowhand on edge. Along the Goodnight-Loving Trail at Horsehead Crossing on the Pecos, the first reliable water after seventy-nine agonizing miles across a Texas hell, Charles Goodnight once counted thirteen graves.

"All [were] the result of pistol shots but one," he noted. "I shall never forget the impression made upon me by those lonely graves, where rested cowboys killed in battle with one another after having fallen out while crossing the long stretch without water."

Between the Middle Concho and Horsehead Crossing, Goodnight also noted two other graves dug at the barrel of a gun. One may have been that of a cowhand named Ewing, who died in an 1870 scrape with a fellow drover at a water hole known as Mustang Pens or Mustang Ponds.

But the Pecos route wasn't the only trace that nurtured violence like the brood grounds of hell. On the trail to Kansas, a pair of 1872 shoot-outs reportedly claimed ten men, nine of whom died in a single battle near present-day Oklahoma City after two cowboys quarreled over a stake pin.

"We buried the dead men as best we could right there on the prairie," Ben Drake said of the latter skirmish.

Before another Kansas-bound outfit even escaped Texas in 1870, a gunman pumped lead through a drover's chest. The culprit, who identified himself only as Rusty, had hired on under trail boss W. T. "Bill" Jackman near a Llano River crossing.

"He was probably thirty years of age, rather small in stature, roughly dressed, wearing long yellow hair which hung gracefully down over his shoulders, giving him the appearance of a very tough character," wrote Jackman.

Rusty soon proved an excellent drover, but during Jackman's brief absence as the herd neared Fort Griffin, the new hand shot fellow waddy John Rice with a forty-four-caliber Winchester rifle.

"The bullet had passed entirely through the body on the opposite side of the spine from the heart, and blood was flowing from both front and back," recalled Jackman.

Upon his return, the trail boss quickly summoned a Fort Griffin doctor, who considered the case hopeless even as he rushed the victim back to the post hospital. To everyone's amazement, however, Rice not only survived, but recovered fully after a lengthy convalescence. The mysterious Rusty, meanwhile, fled on horseback and was never apprehended.

With a cattle trail often passing through a no man's land beyond the reach of the law, the fate of such a perpetrator sometimes remained a mystery even if witnesses knew his name. One such gunman was Bill Driscoll, a cowhand on an 1881 drive from Texas to Indian Territory. A morose and volatile individual who frequently practiced with a forty-five, Driscoll quickly clashed with mild-mannered and retiring Burt Phelps, a twenty-two-year-old who carried a Bible inscribed by his mother. Further distinguishing himself from the typical cowhand, Phelps was erudite and refined, and Driscoll insolently dubbed him "Mama's Boy."

But Driscoll wasn't satisfied with mere insults; he seemed bent on luring Phelps into a gunfight. The latter man, however, always shrugged off the provocation, expressing confidence that his own six-gun prowess was better.

As the outfit camped on the Red River, Driscoll chanced to be nearby when Phelps tossed an armful of wood on the fire. A coal flew up, branding Driscoll in the face. Enraged, he reached for his revolver, but Phelps beat him to the draw and disarmed him long enough to confiscate the shells.

Humiliated, Driscoll plotted revenge as the herd marched on to the DHK range, where the drovers attended a dance. About midnight, Ed Bannister called in through a window and asked Phelps for his revolver; a wolf was on the prowl, Bannister explained, and someone wanted to kill it. Phelps obliged his friend, never realizing that the third party was Driscoll and that the gunman would remove the shells before returning it via the unsuspecting Bannister.

The next day when Phelps and his nemesis crossed paths at a water hole, Driscoll went for his six-shooter. Again, Phelps was quicker, but the firing pin of his weapon snapped against empty cylinders as the gunman took careful aim. An instant later, Phelps was dead.

One report held that Driscoll met his own judgment on the Red River, another that he escaped to New Mexico and became a sheep man; in the fog of the Old West, truth was often as great a casualty as a gunshot victim. As for Phelps, cowhands selected a gentle hill sentineling the Red River for his final resting place.

"With hats in hand, [we] tried to say a prayer," recalled Fred Sutton, who evidently helped bury him. "And failing, [our] eyes dimmed with tears, one member on his knees, with eyes raised to heaven, said, 'Oh, God, look down on this Thy child.'"

Even absent the rigors of the trail as impetus, gunplay could evoke burial scenes just as touching. One danger came from cattle rustlers, whose intent in filling the air with lead usually had less to do with killing than with intimidating or escaping neck-stretchings.

As a pair of cowboys guarded a W Ranch herd in the Pecos country of Texas one night in the late 1890s or early 1900s, strangers approached on horseback and engaged them in conversation. Their attention diverted, the cowhands didn't realize it was a trap until more riders swooped out of the night. Overwhelmed and bound with rawhide, the two herders could only wallow on the ground as the rustlers fled with two hundred twenty-five beeves.

When the nighthawks failed to return to the chuck wagon at daybreak, cowhands undertook a search that lingered throughout the day. Too late to take up the rustlers' trail, the waddies located the missing men. The next morning, the foreman and six cowboys finally gigged their broncs down a trace already more than a day old.

Overtaking even a choused herd should have been easy for unburdened riders, but fifty miles from the W range they lost the trail. Thereafter, they could only cling to a general course with the help of scattered reports of a W herd headed east.

The chase carried the cowboys all the way to Menard County, where they enlisted the aid of the sheriff and his deputies in surrounding the rustlers' camp. Facing prison, the thieves could have chosen to fight, but fortunately for the W riders and lawmen, they surrendered without a shot.

On other occasions, though, rustlers showed no reluctance to opening fire, if for no other reason than to discourage pursuit. Along the Pecos near Monahans, Texas, in December 1904, J. B. Miller of the Keithly Ranch rode upon a calf tied in the brush. Recognizing a plot to steal the animal surreptitiously, Miller hid and waited. As evening fell, two men rode up, only to sight the cowboy and spook. As they raised dust in flight, Miller shouted a demand that they halt, but the whiz of bullets was the only response.

Returning fire, Miller felled one of the horses, but the downed man scrambled up behind his cohort, and the two continued to flee on a horse carrying double. As Miller gave chase, his bronc spilled hard and the impact knocked the cowboy senseless. He had failed to get a clear look at the scoundrels, and by the time he regained his wits they were gone.

The injuries sustained by HAT Ranch cowhands in a New Mexico rustling incident between 1911 and 1913 were considerably greater. After a herd stampeded in a hailstorm, waddies tallied a loss of eighty-five head, prompting Earnest Cook, Jeff Cowden, and Tom Ogles to set out in pursuit. Soon they discovered horse tracks in the trace and realized that rustlers had seized the animals.

All through that day and on into another, the cowhands clung to the trail, and at the end of the second day they reached the mouth of a canyon that framed three riders within revolver range. Cowden was in the lead as the HAT boys charged, only to face a sudden rain of bullets from the fleeing rustlers. A slug ripped through Cowden's ankle, then another through his collarbone.

"He was spilling considerable blood after the second hit, and we called to him, demanding that he drop behind," narrated Cook, who avoided death by mere inches when lead sailed through his hat. "But he paid us no mind and kept on riding and shooting that six-gun."

Finally, the cowboys' gunfire plugged one rustler in the leg and another in the arm, taking the fight out of the thieves. Pulling rein, they whirled their horses and threw up their hands in surrender.

"What are you fellows going to do with us?" pressed a concerned rustler as the HAT boys confiscated their weapons.

"Take you into Roswell and turn you over to the law," one replied.

The rustler was relieved. "Well, that'll be fine—we don't care for rope parties."

The thieves—two of whom identified themselves as Al Jennings and Clay Foster, respectively—served thirteen-month sentences, while the dollar-a-day cowhands split a five-hundred-dollar reward from a cattleman's association.

Apart from the threat of rustlers, a ranch could be the setting for killings over matters as innocent as a prank or as serious as ownership of a small empire. In the Huerfano River country of Colorado in the nineteenth century, Henry Tiel and two other cowboys playfully instructed a greenhorn to enter a particular room in a boarding house and make himself comfortable. The naive tenderfoot did exactly that, but when the rightful tenant, a Mrs. Grubb, returned to find an uninvited guest in her bed, she administered a severe tongue-lashing and chased him out.

Later relating the incident to the cowhands, the greenhorn joined them in laughter, but he wasn't so affable when they decided to shoot holes in his derby hat.

"A joke's a joke," he argued, "but there's no sense ruining a good hat."

Conceding only a little, Tiel drew his six-gun and emptied it at the greenhorn's feet, forcing him to dance a jig. In a knee-jerk reaction, the greenhorn yanked a pistol from his vest and killed the cowhand.

In the opposite extreme, cowman Henry Green murdered his European partner over their joint claim to a Texas cattle operation along the Pecos near old Fort Lancaster. To explain the man's abrupt disappearance, Green told everyone that he had acquired his partner's interest and that the immigrant had returned to Germany. Green eventually relocated to New Mexico and hired on with a ranch, where he dropped to a fatal slug in an altercation with his boss.

"You've killed me," Green muttered with his last breath, "but if I had my gun, I'd get you."

Years later in a secluded canyon along the lower Pecos, hunters stumbled on a skeleton that investigators identified as the remains of the murdered immigrant. Long after Green had joined his old partner in death, it was obvious that justice had found its own way to be served.

Money was also a factor in a ranch killing at White Lake near Lubbock, Texas. Seeking the return of a horse that a foreman held as security against a debt, a neighboring manager rode up to a bunk-house with several cowboys, including J. F. "Red Horse" Henderson. After the opposing foreman came out, the two bosses negotiated, but when words couldn't settle the matter they used their fists. As a mere boy sprang from his horse to separate the two, the foreman shouted into the house for help, and a man rushed out and fell upon the young cowhand.

Suddenly the brawl turned deadly.

"Another fellow appeared in the doorway with a Winchester and pulled down on us all," remembered Henderson. "Our boss didn't take time to get his horse but broke away on foot as fast as he could run. The next shot killed the boy, and as he dropped to the ground, I turned down on my horse's side, put spurs to him, and was gone."

Henderson slowed just long enough to pick up his foreman, then the two fled the ricocheting bullets and made it safely to their home ranch. Rounding up every available cowhand, they returned in force with a wagon to retrieve the victim's body.

"He was still lying in the front yard, and not a man showed up as we lifted him to the wagon and started on our long, slow journey to Snyder, Texas, for burial," related Henderson. "His father and mother lived near Snyder and had no thought but what he was well and happy until we arrived with the body."

The motive in a 1913 killing on a Big Bend ranch in Texas is more clouded. A thirteen-year-old boy with aspirations to be a cowboy had drifted into the region and hired on with Henry Lemmons and his two adult sons, Millard and Will. From a tent headquarters at the northwest end of the Dead Horse Mountains, the Lemmons clan grazed fifteen hundred goats. As Will bent over a Dutch oven on April 13, the teenager took a bead with a thirty-thirty Winchester and fired. The slug tore through Will's right nipple, passed through the underside of his chin, severed his tongue, and exited through his cheek.

As the elder Lemmons raced for the tent to seize a gun, the boy fatally shot him where his suspenders crossed. Millard, too, bolted for the tent, but the teenager fired another fatal bullet that draped him across his father's body.

Evidently presuming all three men dead, the assailant made his way to the Boquillas road and tried to flag down a mail hack. But the boy's Winchester and demeanor alarmed the wagoner, who proceeded to whip the mules into a run. The teenager emptied the rifle at the fleeing man but succeeded only in putting a couple of holes in the hack.

Under a dehydrating sun, the boy trudged across the desert to a shack at Bone Springs and pounded on a door with a gap at the bottom.

"Let me in! Let me in!" he cried. "I want some water!"

But the occupants, including Pete Valenzuela, weren't about to unbolt for a wild-eyed kid brandishing a thirty-thirty.

"Stick your gun under the door!" Valenzuela ordered.

"Ain't got no cartridges anyhow," said the teenager, sliding the rifle under.

The only weapon in the shack was an empty shotgun, but when Valenzuela opened the door, he used it to bluff the boy. Soon, he had the teenager secured with baling wire.

While a goatherd at Bone Springs arranged for a U.S. Army truck to transport the prisoner to the authorities in Marathon, the wounded Will Lemmons staggered half-dead across a broiling wasteland to Maravillas Creek and the Pitaya Hill Ranch, forty miles from the scene of the shootings. Thomas Henderson, who was only five at the time, saw Lemmons approaching and summoned his father from the house.

"He's sure bloody, all over," Thomas told him. "Clothes are tore and full of thorns."

The elder Henderson rushed out and found Lemmons barely able to communicate.

"It shot that tongue in two, and he couldn't talk," Thomas recalled in 1990. "You could understand some words—he didn't have no water; he wanted a drink of water."

The elder Henderson helped the wounded man into the house, where Thomas's mother tended him as best she could.

"He had a piece of gum hanging out with three teeth on it and some bone," remembered Thomas. "Mama got shears and whacked that gum off, throwed it through the door, and an old chicken grabbed it and run off. Then she strained some soup and poured it down his throat."

As for the assailant, he would tell authorities only that he had committed his heinous crime because the Lemmons men had refused to repair his shoes.

Like the Hendersons, any resident of a remote ranch never knew when a cowhand in need would come along. When A. G. Anderson and his bride located on a lower Pecos ranch, he gave her permission to loan anything but his horse, saddle, or gun. Nevertheless, when a stranger rode up on an exhausted horse during Anderson's absence and asked for a fresh mount, she obliged. Someone had been shot, the stranger told her, and he needed the horse to summon a doctor from Sheffield.

When the rider returned a half hour later, the bronc was so lathered that the woman required him to walk the animal a full hour to prevent stiffness. Long after the stranger rode away on his own horse, she learned the truth: He had shot the man himself at a dance, and his purpose in borrowing a fresh mount was to delay the doctor long enough for the victim to die. The physician, however, had taken a shortcut across a mountain and unwittingly had avoided the stranger.

Few settings were as peaceful to a cowboy as a chuck wagon campfire, around which he might gobble up a nourishing meal, drink black coffee, and share wild horse tales before seeking his bedroll. Sometimes, though, tragedy entered this cowboy's Eden, just as it did one night in 1915 as twenty-year-old Richard Murphy and his pal Henry Ford warmed before the flames on the Turkey Track, sixty-five miles northwest of Tucson, Arizona.

"We were . . . swapping yarns, and I was sitting at the side of Ford, with my right arm resting on his shoulder," recalled Murphy. "He and I was singing. We had reached about the end of the song and had finished the words '*Take me back to the open range*' when a shot was fired from out of the darkness."

The bullet passed through Murphy's sleeve and exploded against the base of Ford's skull, killing him even as he fell forward.

The shooter escaped into the night, but the Turkey Track boys presumed him to be Henry Lewis, with whom Ford had a feud. A week later the grief-torn Murphy, who had come so close to dying himself, quit the outfit and returned to his native Texas.

The Lone Star State fostered its own share of fatal shootings, even as late as the mid-1920s when gunfire rocked the White and Swearington range near Big Spring. Springing partly from racial tensions of the day, the incident involved a high-tempered Mexican cook and a white cowboy.

When fifteen-year-old "Jim Ed Rowden" dragged a beef to the wagon so the cook could slaughter it, he overheard the Mexican national say that he intended to kill the cowhand. Rowden (who requested his real name be withheld) immediately reported the threat to the unsuspecting man.

"It'll be a cold day in hell when that Mexican does that," responded the cowpoke, who kept a thirty-thirty on his saddle.

Three weeks later, the cook allegedly insulted the cowhand's wife, leading to the Mexican's dismissal. With camp located far off the beaten path, the cowhand agreed to drive him to town in a Dodge auto, but he had second thoughts after traveling only a short distance. Slamming on the brakes, he whirled to the Mexican and ordered him out. First, he would beat the hell out of him, the waddy snarled, then leave him afoot.

When the two men climbed out, the cook pulled a knife with a double-edged eleven-inch blade and charged. Startled, the cowboy drew a forty-five-caliber six-shooter, but the muzzle didn't deter the enraged Mexican. He continued to rush the cowhand, who was reluctant to shoot and could only retreat.

"He was just runnin' around and around that car," related Rowden, who first saw the events from a hundred fifty yards away as he approached on horseback with other hastening riders.

When the horsemen pulled rein at the scene, one man jumped off his mount between the combatants and seized the cowhand's revolver, hoping to prevent a killing. His peacemaking effort failed, though, for the Mexican now redirected his attack to this second cowboy, who was equally reluctant to fire.

"He was runnin' backwards throwin' his hands up, and the Mexican cut him on both wrists, arms, and hands pretty bad," narrated Rowden.

Desperate, the cowboy pumped two slugs into the assailant's stomach, but the crazed man wouldn't be stopped. Suddenly, the cowhand tripped and fell backward over a bush, leaving him no choice but to shoot for the chest as the Mexican pounced on him with the knife.

The final slug found the attacker's heart.

"The Mexican just fell over on him," remembered Rowden. "You never seen a long-legged man kick so in his life like that guy did gettin' him off him."

The wagon boss, protective of young Rowden, spun to him. "Jim Ed, you get the hell out of here!" he ordered.

As soon as Rowden did so, the cowboys draped the Mexican's body across a horse, led the animal to a mott of chittam trees, and committed the corpse to a hidden grave.

Still, word somehow filtered all the way into Mexico, spurring the dead man's two brothers into trekking to the ranch a month later to exact revenge. A shoot-out at a rock house between the involved cowhands and the brothers failed to wreak casualties, but it served to break virtually everyone's silence about the cook's death. Young Rowden alone kept quiet, and no one implicated him during the subsequent investigation. Authorities ruled the killing self-defense, but the cover-up netted a trio of cowhands two-year suspended sentences.

Inasmuch as Indian depredations of an earlier era were concerned, the only justice was that meted out by the force of arms. For decades, innumerable skirmishes erupted between cowboys going about their jobs and warrior societies seeking glory in battle. The mind-sets of the two groups were entirely different, and few cowhands could muster empathy for a people such as the Comanches who gladly rode a thousand miles to make war for war's sake alone. In a very real sense, the cattle industry helped give warrior societies exactly what they wanted—a stage on which to thrill in combat or die in the process and thus escape the infirmities of old age.

Nevertheless, it was a drama in which no cowboy wanted a part.

Reaching the North Canadian with a Wichita-bound herd in 1870, E. P. Byler came upon a fresh grave with a headboard inscribed *Killed by Indians*. "I do not know who the unfortunate victim could have been," he reflected many years later, "but these graves were not uncommon."

Indeed, forgotten graves throughout the West still testify to the price many cowhands paid for their work ethic in the face of flying arrows. The story of two Central Texas punchers of the late 1860s, Albert K. Erwin and his partner, continues to speak powerfully of not only the uncertainty of a cowboy's life during the Indian wars, but the unfathomable role played by Providence in who endured and who perished.

"He and I were riding side by side, and we were, as usual those days, scanning the territory to locate any lurking Indian," remembered eighty-eight-year-old Erwin in the twilight of his years. "Not a sign or sight of one did we see. Suddenly an arrow hit on the top of his skull and entered his head."

The odds against an arcing arrow catching a moving rider so precisely from a distance were astronomical, but it had happened.

Erwin E. Smith paying his respects at a cowboy's grave on the OR Ranch in Arizona in 1909. (E. E. Smith Collection, Nita Stewart Haley Memorial Library, Midland, Texas)

While Erwin survived to ride far into another century, his partner fell dead mere feet away, his boots not only still on, but firmly planted in the stirrups.

Assuredly, no one of vigor and purpose would have longed for life's end—not when there were so many trails left to ride—but if death had to come by way of violence, a dedicated cowboy couldn't have asked for better.

The world is all behind us, but by God, we are leaving a lot behind us to show we was here once.

—Teddy Blue Abbott, cowhand

Bibliography

Author's Interviews with pre-1932 Cowboys of Texas and New Mexico

Alexander, Hewitt, by telephone, Jasper, Texas, 16 October 1990.

Armentrout, Steve "Slim," Fort Stockton, Texas, 1 September 1989.

Arrott, Clarence, Bronte, Texas, by telephone, 13 October 1990.

Baker, Louis, Bronte, Texas, 14 February 1990.

Beauchamp, Marvin, Midland, Texas, 8 September 1989.

Blasingame, Tom, JA Ranch, Armstrong County, Texas, 26 July 1989.

Boren, Walter, Post, Texas, 8 August 1990.

Boykin, Gaston, Comanche, Texas, 13 September 1989.

Brice, Lee Loyd, Ector County, Texas, 13 August 1990.

Broughton, William Earnest, by telephone, Kimble County, Texas, 23 February 1990.

Calcote, Bob, by telephone, Midkiff, Texas, 14 October 1990.

Cauble, Jack, by telephone, Vega, Texas, 13 October 1990.

Coggins, Otis D., Alpine, Texas, 3 March 1990.

Cone, Charlie, by telephone, Abilene, Texas, 16 October 1990.

Davidson, Bill, Big Spring, Texas, 22 September 1989.

Davis, Alton, Coleman, Texas, 14 February 1990.

Davis, L. E., Tom Green County, Texas, 15 February 1990.

Davis, Ralph, Sterling City, Texas, 4 March and 22 July 1989.

Davis, Vance, Big Spring, Texas, 22 September 1989.

Derrick, Frank, Clarendon, Texas, 26 July 1989.

Doran, Lewis, Monahans, Texas, 20 February 1990.

Drennan, Charlie, Sterling City, Texas, 26 November 1990.

Duncan, Tom, by telephone, Brady, Texas, 16 October 1990.

Dunnahoo, Alphonzo, by telephone, Loraine, Texas, 18 October 1990.

Durham, Will, Sterling County, Texas, 25 February 1989.

Eddins, L. B. "Bill," Kermit, Texas, 5 September 1989.

Fairweather, J. E. "Jim," Midland, Texas, 1 March 1989.

George, Olan, Fort Stockton, Texas, 1 September 1989.

Green, W. R., Marathon, Texas, 9 February 1990.

Griffith, Lonnie, Big Spring, Texas, 30 March 1983.

Hall, Weir, by telephone, Mertzon, Texas, 31 October 1990.

Henderson, Thomas B., Marathon, 9 February 1990.

Hernandez, Leonard, Crane, Texas, 29 August 1989.

Hoelscher, Walter, Olfen, Texas, 29 June 1990.

Hooper, Marvin, Crane County, Texas, 13 November 1989.

Kinser, L., San Angelo, Texas, 24 August 1989.

Lambert, Joe, Hobbs, New Mexico, 6 July 1989.

Lane, Carl, by telephone, Robert Lee, Texas, 14 October 1990.

Laughlin, Ted W., Midland County, Texas, 7 February 1990.

Loeffler, S. M. "Si," Sonora, Texas, 30 June 1990.

Mankin, Green, Mills County, Texas, 14 September 1989.

Mayes, Hudson "Bud," Ozona, Texas, 22 February 1990 and 30 April 1991.

McClellan, Fred, Colorado City, Texas, 6 September 1989.

McEntire, George H. Jr. "Little George," San Angelo, Texas, 15 July 1989.

Midkiff, Tyson, Rankin, Texas, 9 August 1989; by telephone, Rankin, 11 December 1990; Rankin, 29 April 1991.

Murrah, Buck, by telephone, Del Rio, Texas, 18 October 1990.

Murrell, John L., by telephone, Earth, Texas, 16 October 1990.

Northcutt, J. E. "Shorty," Spade Ranch, Mitchell County, Texas, 6 September 1989.

Owens, Claude, Fort Stockton, Texas, 2 March 1990.

Parisher, Tom William, Ozona, Texas, 22 February 1990.

Pate, Jack, by telephone, Albany, Texas, 10 March 1990.

Patterson, Paul, Crane, Texas, 1 April 1983; Castle Gap, Texas, 21 June 1989; Hobbs, New Mexico, 13 November 1989; Alpine, Texas, 2 and 3 March 1990; Lubbock, Texas, 1 June 1990; Castle Gap, 23 June 1990; Crane, 29 April 1991; by telephone, Crane, 28 September 1992; by telephone, Pecos, Texas, 20 January 1998; Centralia Station, Texas, 30 October 1998; Upton County, Texas, 2 November 1998; by telephone, Crane, 14 January 1999; Upton County, 26 April 1999; Crane, 12 August, 2004; by telephone, Crane, 2 October and 24 November 2004.

Poage, Douglas, Ruidoso Downs, New Mexico, 28 September 1990.

Poage, Walton, Rankin, Texas, 30 August 1989.

Powers, Ted, San Angelo, Texas, 23 August 1989.

Proctor, Leonard, Midland, Texas, 2 March 1989.

Rankin, Billy, Rankin, Texas, 9 August 1989 and 29 April 1991.

Reding, Gid, Fort Stockton, Texas, 1 September 1989.

Reed, Max, by telephone, Goldsmith, Texas, 16 October 1990.

Renfro, Willard, Ballinger, Texas, 14 February 1990.

Rooney, Francis, by telephone, Marathon, Texas, 14 October 1990.

Shields, Bill, by telephone, Wellington, Texas, 13 October 1990.

Smith, Charles Kenneth, Marfa, Texas, 12 February 1990.

Sparks, Orval, by telephone, San Angelo, Texas, 14 November 1990.

Stevens, John, by telephone, Texas Panhandle, 13 October 1990.

Stokes, Aubrey, by telephone, Vealmoor, Texas, 13 October 1990.

Stroup, J. R. "Jim," Quitaque, Texas, 27 July 1989.

Taylor, Troy "Jones," Silverton, Texas, 26 July 1989.

Townsend, Bill, by telephone, Vera, Texas, 22 July 1995; Odessa, Texas, 3 August 1995.

Villalba, Chon, Fort Stockton, Texas, 9 February 1990.

Vines, P. O. "Slim," Crane, Texas, 16 August 1989.

Whatley, Wood, by telephone, Quanah, Texas, 10 March 1990.

Wilson, Maynard "Fish," Quitaque, Texas, 27 July 1989.

Witt, Jim, Loving, New Mexico, 17 July 1993; by telephone, Loving, 22 July 1995.

Yeary, Frank, Silverton, Texas, 26 July 1989.

Young, Seth, by telephone, Uvalde, Texas, 23 February 1990.

Bibliography

Interview Transcripts, 1936–1940, Library of Congress, Manuscript Division, WPA Federal Writers' Project Collection

Adams, Jap

Anderson, A. G.

Anderson, Andre Jorgenson

Angermiller, William Riley

Ater, Jonathan Sanford "Toad"

Barrow, Avery N.

Benard, J. P.

Bennett, Jacob

Biggs, William B.

Blalock, S. H.

"Bones"

Brady, William Walter

Brown, J. M.

Buchannan, J. S.

Burnes, Dave E.

Byler, J. H. "Jake"

Campbell, Brook

Campbell, Hugh

"Canyon City Folkways"

Cape, James

Cardwell, O. T.

Carr, W. J. D.

"Charles C. Roberts and I Were Married"

Childers, James

Cody, Harry Buffington

Cook, Earnest

Cook, H. P.

Cowan, P. L.

Cowan, Troy B.

Cox, L. M.

Crawford, Ed

Crittendon, Will

Cumbie, Irvin

Currie, W. B.

Davis, John S.

Dayton, William F.

Dobbs, W. L.

Driver, M. F. "Mart"

Erwin, Albert K.

Fergenson, Gaston

Flor, M. C. de la

Fuller, John H.

Fuller, Robert Lee

Gardenhire, J. T.

Garrett, A. M.

Garrett, Tom

Graftenreid, Buster de

Hale, Andrew Jackson

Hardeman, John M.

Hart, Luther C.

Henderson, J. F.

Hess, J. C.

Hines, T. E.

Hooks, Bones

"How Snaky Joe Got His Name"

Hurley, J. H.

Jolly, Jesse

Jones, Edward F.

Keen, Robert W.

Kellis, W. F.

Ketchum, Mrs. Helen

Kilgore, Martin Henry

Kinchlow, Ben

Knight, William S.

Law, Mrs. Elvira Hobbs

Bibliography

Little, Robert William
Ludwig, R. E.
Maines, John Jr.
Manuel, M. C.
Mathis, James W.
May, Dave
Mayes, Ben
McAulay, W. L.
McClure, Tom
McCrohan, Eugene
McGregor, Eddie
McGuire, James
McKinney, T. N.
McNeill, William
Mills, Tom
Miskimon, Mrs. Ben McCulloch Earl Van Dorn
Mooney, James M.
Mooring, J. G.
Morgan, Mrs. Tom
Morrison, Walter R.
Murphy, Richard
Newman, Lois
Ogden, George
Oglesby, W. E.
"On July 21, 1879, I Was Married"
Owens, William
Patrick, Riley
Pearson, B. R.
Phillips, Richard C.
Pickett, Winfield Thomas
Posey, Willie Addison
Preist, William A.
Rattan, Dr. A. S.
Rawlings, Ed
Rhodes, W. L.

Richardson, Raymond

Riley, Edward W.

Robinson, John

Rogers, Sam J.

Schroeder, Gus

Shannon, J. D.

Sinclair, Daniel Boone

Smith, J. H.

Smith, L. E.

Smith, R. W.

Smith, William A.

Snow, Tom J.

Steen, E. E.

Stetler, C. E. Jr.

Stiers, George S.

Tarter, J. L.

Thomas, W. H.

Tinney, W. A.

Townsen, A. P.

Walker, H. P.

Walkup, J. R.

Washington, Sam James

Watts, Neal S.

Whetaker, Fred W.

Woody, J. J.

Wootan, F. J.

Yardley, J. H.

Young, Henry

U.S. Works Administration Interview Transcripts, Colorado Historical Society, Denver, Colorado

Edwards, Wilson, to Margaret Merrill

Farr, Charles J., to B. B. Guthrie

Thatcher, William, to A. K. Richeson

Bibliography

Interview Transcripts, Nita Stewart Haley Memorial Library, Midland, Texas

Aten, Ira, to J. Evetts Haley, El Centro, California, 26 February 1928.

Denby, Al, Mrs. Bob Duke File.

Elliston, Gene, Mrs. Bob Duke File.

Goodnight, Charles, to J. Evetts Haley, Clarendon, Texas, 5 June 1925 and 8 April 1927.

Hayes, Mose, to J. Evetts Haley, San Antonio, Texas, 3 March 1935.

Jennings, W., Mrs. Bob Duke File.

McCanless, J. E., to J. Evetts Haley, Dalhart, Texas, 21 March 1928.

McClure, Harrison, to J. Evetts Haley, Gonzales, Texas, 9 September 1935.

Moore, J. E., to J. Evetts Haley, Dalhart, Texas, 8 November 1927.

Roberson, G. W., to J. Evetts Haley, Vega, Texas, 30 June 1926.

Roberts, Jim W., to J. Evetts Haley, Lake Arthur (Hagerman), New Mexico, 24 June 1927.

Scott, F. A., to J. Evetts Haley, Canyon, Texas, 26 June and 17 November 1926, 11 June 1935, and 16 September 1945.

Smiley, J. A., Mrs. Bob Duke File.

Smith, C. R., to J. Evetts Haley, Hereford, Texas, 11 August 1927.

Sneed, Arch, Mrs. Bob Duke File.

Turnbow, T. A., Mrs. Bob Duke File.

Withers, Mark, to J. Evetts Haley, Lockhart, Texas, 8 October 1932.

Letters, Manuscripts, Diaries

Abbott, Teddy Blue, to A. B. Blocker, 26 May 1931, Nita Stewart Haley Memorial Library, Midland, Texas.

Abbott, Teddy Blue, to Frost Woodhull, 29 May, 17 June, 2 July, and 18 November 1931, Haley Library.

Baker, James H., diary, Haley Library.

Burgess, Perry A., Memoirs 1866–1868 (diary), Norlin Library Archives, University of Colorado, Boulder, Colorado.

Burns, R. C., manuscript, Haley Library.

Caldwell, Samuel Jr., MacMillan's Ranche, River's Bend, Colorado, to his mother, 1 July 1878, Samuel Caldwell Jr. Papers, 1878, Special Collections, Colorado College Charles Leaming Tutt Library, Colorado Springs, Colorado.

Caldwell, Samuel Jr., diary, Samuel Caldwell Jr. Papers, 1878, Special Collections, Colorado College Charles Leaming Tutt Library.

Cochran, W. C., "A Trip to Kansas," secured by J. Evetts Haley, 25 October 1926, Haley Library.

Cochran, W. C., "A Trip to Montana in 1869," Haley Library.

Connell, W. D., Hereford, Texas, to his wife, 27 May 1903, Special Collections, University of Texas of the Permian Basin, Odessa, Texas.

Hancock, W. B., "American Aristocrat," dictated to Bertha Monagin Hancock, winter 1934, Haley Library.

Hayes, Edward G., ZA Ranch, to Joseph Byron Hayes, 5 May 1887, Edward Graham Hayes Papers, Special Collections, Colorado College Charles Leaming Tutt Library.

Loy, M. H., manuscript dated 7 January 1930, Haley Library.

Oden, B. A., "Early Cowboy Days in New Mexico and Texas," Haley Library.

Woodhull, Frost, to *The Cattleman*, 6 June 1931, quoting from letters from Teddy Blue Abbott to Woodhull, Haley Library.

Books

Abbott, E. C., and Helena Huntington Smith. *We Pointed Them North*. Norman: University of Oklahoma Press, 9th printing, 1989.

Adams, Ramon F. *Western Words: A Dictionary of the Range, Cow Camp and Trail*. Norman: University of Oklahoma Press, 1944.

Dearen, Patrick. *A Cowboy of the Pecos*. Plano, Tex: Republic of Texas Press, 1997.

———. *Halff of Texas*. Austin, Tex: Eakin Press, 2000.

———. *The Last of the Old-Time Cowboys*. Plano, Tex: Republic of Texas Press, 1998.

Bibliography

Gard, Wayne. *The Chisholm Trail*. Norman: University of Oklahoma Press, 9th printing, 1988.

Haley, J. Evetts. *Charles Goodnight, Cowman and Plainsman*. Norman: University of Oklahoma Press, 10th printing, 1987.

Hunter, J. Marvin, ed. and compiler. *The Trail Drivers of Texas*. Austin: University of Texas Press, reprint, 1985.

Townley, Mary Fay Borland. *Life in the Early West and on the Chisolm Trail*. Privately printed, 1970.

Newspaper

Texas Live Stock Journal (sometimes styled *Texas Stock and Farm Journal* and *Texas Stockman-Journal*), 1883, 1890, 1903, 1904.

Index

Note: Page numbers in italics indicate photos.

Miller, J. B., 150–51
Miller brothers, 13
Mills, G. W., 89
Mills, Tom, 59
Missouri River, 125
Monahans, Texas, 150
Montvale, Texas, 81, 89
Mooring, J. G., 100–102
Morrison, Walter R., 68–69
Moseur and Mendel Ranch (Texas),
   23
Motley County, Texas, 40
Moye, Babe, 125, 130
Muleshoe Ranch (Texas), 59
Murphy, Richard, 156
Murrah, Buck, 71
Murrell, John L., 9, 14
Mustang Pens, 147
Mustang Ponds, 147

N Bar N Ranch, 126
Nance, Jerry M., 89, 127
Newton, Jim, 126
North Canadian River, 127, 158
North Concho River, 89
North Platte River, 122, 126
Northcutt, Shorty, 12, 24, 45, 54–55
NUN Ranch (Texas), 103

Oden, B. A., 102–3, 120
Odessa, Texas, 63
Ogallala, Nebraska, 122
Ogles, Tom, 151–52
Oglesby, W. E., 109–10
OH Triangle Ranch (Texas), 30
Olive, Ira, 147
Open A Ranch (Texas), 144
OR Ranch (Arizona), 1, 55, 141, 159
OS Ranch (Texas), 56
Owens, Claude, 28
Owens, Jake, 104
Owens, William, 107
Ozona, Texas, 80, 134, 136

Pareco River (Arizona), 107
Parisher, Tom, 15, 21, 23, 55

Patterson, John, 28, 54
Patterson, Paul, 15, 29, 39, 53, 54,
   63, 77, 79–81
Pecos River, 2, 23, 38, 61, 86, 112,
   114, 120, 136, 138, 147, 150,
   152–53, 155
Penwell, Texas, 69
Pettit, Carl, 136
Phelps, Burt, 148–49
Phillips, Richard C., 37
Pierce, Bob, 59
Pierce, Shanghai, 13
Piree, John W., 140
Pitaya Hill Ranch (Texas), 155
Platte River, 118
Poage, Douglas, 30, 46, 53, 145
Poage, Walton, 6–7, 55–56
Porter, Buck, 62–63
Powers, Ted, 47, 66, 135, 135, 136,
   138
Preist, William A., 39, 114
Proctor, Foy, 41
Proctor, Leonard, 28
Pulliam, M. B. "Nub," 110

Rankin, Billy, 30, 39, 41, 81
Rawlings, Ed, 120
Red (cowhand), 114
Red River, 85, 118, 120–22, 125–26,
   128, 130, 149
Red River Station, 94
Reding, Gid, 28, 33
Rice, John, 148
Richardson, Raymond, 5
Rio Grande (Texas), 59, 112, 123–
   24, 144
Roberson, G. W., 142
Robinson, Allen, 21
Robuck, E. A. "Berry," 69, 90, 123
Rogers, Sam J., 9
Roswell, New Mexico, 151
Rusty (cowhand), 148

Salt Creek (Texas), 59
Salt Fork of the Red River, 91
San Antonio, Texas, 105, 107

White and Swearington Ranch
(Texas), 156
White Lake (Texas), 153
Wichita, Kansas, 158
Wiggins, Red, 82–83
Williams, Tony, 128
Wilson, Fish, 13, 15, 54, 58–59, 64–
65, 133
Wilson, Jim, 92–93
Wilson, "One-Armed Bill," 74
Withers, G. B., 95
Withers, M. A. "Mark," 86, 95,
106–7, 121–22
Witt, Jim, 23

X Ranch (Texas), 77
XIT Ranch (Texas), 16, 120, 142,
145

Yardley, J. H., 57–58
Yeary, Frank, 6, 18, 47–48, 140–41
Yellowstone River, 118, 126
Yiser, Jimmy, 79
YO Ranch (Texas), 62
Young, John, 129
Young, Seth, 7, 22–23

ZH Ranch (Indian Territory), 104